Personification
in Eighteenth-Century
English Poetry

PERSONIFICATION
IN EIGHTEENTH-CENTURY
ENGLISH POETRY

By CHESTER F. CHAPIN

1968
OCTAGON BOOKS, INC.
New York

Reprinted 1968

by special arrangement with Chester F. Chapin

OCTAGON BOOKS, INC.
175 FIFTH AVENUE
NEW YORK, N. Y. 10010

LIBRARY OF CONGRESS CATALOG CARD NUMBER: 68-17369

Printed in U.S.A. by
NOBLE OFFSET PRINTERS, INC.
NEW YORK 3, N. Y.

To Karl E. Prickett

Acknowledgments

I AM DEEPLY INDEBTED to Professors James L. Clifford and Marjorie Nicolson of Columbia University for many helpful criticisms and suggestions. My thanks are due to Professor George W. Boyd of Mississippi State College for help in the preparation of the index.

CHESTER F. CHAPIN

Mississippi State College
April, 1955

Contents

Introduction

THE PRESENT STUDY of eighteenth-century personification is concerned with the personified abstraction rather than with personifications of material objects. No distinction, however, is made between abstractions representing more or less palpable, external phenomena, such as Evening, Spring, Opera, Agriculture—and personifications of moral principles, faculties of mind, passions, or states of being, such as Honor, Fancy, Anger, Solitude, and the like. Pathetic fallacies, however—by which is meant the attribution of personal characteristics to material objects such as rivers, trees, or animals—have been excluded from consideration.

Recent criticism which has had to do, directly or indirectly, with eighteenth-century personification may be divided into two broad categories according to the extent of the critic's concern with practice as distinguished from theory, or with theory as opposed to practice. Those who have examined the figure as it actually appears in certain eighteenth-century poems have not attempted a systematic study of critical theory in relation to poetic practice, while those interested in critical theory have not attempted a systematic examination of the ways in which the figure is actually employed in the verse of different eighteenth-century poets. Little attention, accordingly, has been paid to the differences between one sort of personification and another, or to the relationship between different poetic traditions in eighteenth-century verse and the type of personification which appears in that verse. I have felt that an adequate understanding of the figure as it appears in relation to the poetry of the century as a whole could not be attained until these differences were clearly recognized. This study, accordingly, attempts to set the personified abstraction against a background of poetic theory and practice which shall be relevant to eighteenth-century verse in its larger aspects.

It is hoped that this book will be of some interest, not only to specialists in the eighteenth century but to students of the romantic period as well, and to others who may be concerned primarily with the history of English poetics. Poetic figures of speech inevitably reflect the larger world of which they are a part, and while I have been concerned with the personified abstraction and "not another thing," I have not found it possible or desirable to give an account of the figure without reference to topics of more general interest.

It is assumed in this study that no figure of speech is good or bad in itself, and that success or failure in the use of any literary device cannot be predicated on the basis of *a priori* judgments concerning the inherent value of the device itself. This may seem to state the obvious, but during the nineteenth century and later personification was condemned because it made for "abstractness" in poetry, when poetry, it was felt, should deal only with concrete particulars. This derogatory estimate of the figure is reflected in the criticism of Thomas Quayle, whose study of eighteenth-century poetic diction appeared in 1924.[1] Later estimates, such as that of B. H. Bronson,[2] have been more favorable, but if Quayle tends to condemn the figure as such, Bronson goes to the other extreme. He leaves the impression that the values which he properly finds in Johnson's use of the figure in the ode *On the Death of Mr. Robert Levet* represent values which are inherent in the figure itself. But, as E. R. Wasserman has pointed out, personification is "a device of art, not the product of art":[3] its esthetic value depends upon its organic relation to the context in which it appears. Wasserman's thoroughly detailed study is devoted to the purpose of discovering "some of the expectations that personification excited in the mind of the eighteenth-century reader."[4] The qualities in poetry which are most highly valued today are not, in every instance, identical with those most highly valued during the eighteenth century, and it is one of the objects of this study to show how this change in attitude has affected present-day evaluations of the personified abstraction as it appears in eighteenth-century verse.

Studies of critical theory, such as that of Wasserman, have been supplemented in recent years by critical evaluations of the figure as it appears in certain eighteenth-century poems. I owe much in this study to the critical writings of F. R. Leavis and to the discussion of Johnson's poetry which appears in Donald Davie's recent book, *Purity of Diction in English Verse*.[5]

While I am indebted to these and to other modern criticisms,[6] I have sought to do justice to the eighteenth-century point of view. I find that there are, in fact, two different types of eighteenth-century personification—a type which approaches the nature of allegory and a type which shows certain of the characteristics of metaphor. The latter type, it seems to me, is the more valuable, but the former type performed a legitimate function to the extent that it satisfied certain expectations which eighteenth-century readers brought to poetry. While there is no sharp line of division to be drawn between these two sorts of personification, the differences between them have seemed of sufficient importance to justify the organization of this essay into two parts. Part One deals with the allegorical or descriptive type of personification, Part Two with the type "most capable of exerting metaphorical force."[7] I find, moreover, that these two sorts of personification are each of them associated with a different poetic tradition. The metaphorical type is especially suited to the purposes of the neoclassic "poetry of statement," while the allegorical type is especially favored by those mid-century poets who derive much of their inspiration from the minor poems of Milton.

The attitudes toward poetry which lead to an extensive use of the allegorical type of personification lead also to an overemphasis on the figure as "a mechanical device of style"[8] in much mid-

and late eighteenth-century verse. I have sought to trace the development of these attitudes from their early beginnings. Part One, therefore, is roughly chronological. The first chapter deals largely with early eighteenth-century attitudes toward personification, the second with mid-century developments, while chapter V is concerned mainly with late eighteenth-century attitudes toward the figure. Chapter III is devoted to a discussion of the factors responsible for the prevalence of the allegorical type of personification in eighteenth-century verse, while chapter IV contains a critical evaluation of this device as it appears in the verse of Collins and Gray.

Part Two begins with a discussion of attitudes toward poetry held in common by Johnson and Pope, the most talented representatives of a tradition which is found to differ significantly from the poetic tradition described in Part One of the study. Part Two is chiefly critical: I have sought to indicate the values which personification may have when it is employed by poets whose verse bears a more "serious relation to the life of its time"[9] than does the verse of those poets considered in Part One.

Although I distinguish two different sorts of eighteenth-century personification, I find that both types are formed under the influence of those empirical theories of mind which determined contemporary attitudes toward the nature and function of "reason" and "imagination" in poetry. Chapter I, accordingly, is devoted to a discussion of these theories of mind in so far as they are seen to affect eighteenth-century attitudes toward the personified abstraction as a product of "the Poet's Brain."[10]

Part One

ADDISON AND THE EMPIRICAL THEORY
OF IMAGINATION

ALTHOUGH personification has been called one of the hallmarks
of eighteenth-century poetry,[1] it is not as prevalent in the verse
of the earlier poets as in the verse of those writing after 1740.
The poems of the Wartons, Gray, Collins, Mason, and the mid-
century poets generally are proportionately more thickly strewn
with personifications than those of Pope, Swift, Gay, and the
Queen Anne poets, nor does it appear that the popular poets
of the eighties and nineties are any less addicted to the use of the
figure.[2]

This conclusion is confirmed by a consideration of the
eighteenth-century ode, a poetic "kind" conducive in itself to
the use of personification. The figure occurs more frequently in
the ode than in any other contemporary genre with the possible
exception of the professed allegorical poem. Dryden's *Miscellany*
(1648-1709) has no odes to abstractions "and few odes of any
kind," while Dodsley's *Miscellany* (1748-58), which included
"every important poet of the time" except Young, contains
twenty-three addresses to abstractions "and some 40 other odes."
Personified abstractions, says R. D. Havens,

sprinkle the pages of Dodsley's Collection thick as motes that people
the sunbeam. It is simply incredible how many there are, often ten or
fifteen on a page and relatively few pages without at least one.[3]

Personification is prominent also in the poetry of the *Gentleman's
Magazine*. C. D. Yost finds that the mode of personification

present in the odes and in the other forms of poetry printed in this magazine "continued without change to 1780, and beyond to the time of Wordsworth and Byron."[4] In its origins, personification is a classical figure of speech and Yost cites its widespread use in later eighteenth-century poetry as "another proof of the supremacy of . . . neo-classicism" during this period.[5] Certainly, if one thinks simply of the earlier period as "neoclassic" and of the later period as "preromantic," it may be disconcerting to find that personified abstractions occur more frequently in later than in earlier eighteenth-century verse. In attempting to account for this fact, I have thought it best to begin at the beginning. The attitudes toward poetry responsible for the proliferation of personified abstractions in later eighteenth-century verse are to be viewed in the light of accentuated tendencies: in order to gain an adequate understanding of later developments one must see what poets and critics of the early century have to say about the figure. But first, a word about "backgrounds."

The animating metaphor is frequent in the writings of the ancients, in prose as well as in poetry. Eighteenth-century critics refer to isolated examples of the figure in Homer, Virgil, Plato, Horace, and many others. There were, in addition, the numerous personifications of abstract qualities which appeared in the *Tabula* of Cebes and in Prodicus' apologue *The Choice of Hercules*. These pieces, which were included in the curriculum of the schools, had a considerable influence on the eighteenth-century allegorical poem.[6]

The comments of Aristotle, Quintilian, and Longinus showed that personification enjoyed a high measure of esteem among those ancients most renowned in the eighteenth century for critical acumen. Aristotle stressed the value of the animating metaphor as that figure which exhibits "the actions of living creatures . . . attributed to things without life; as when the sword is said to devour."[7] Animation itself is called "the greatest grace of an oration."[8] The comments of Quintilian and Longinus showed that the poet's use of the figure might sometimes achieve the sublime, a quality held to be among the very highest criteria of literary excellence by most eighteenth-century men of letters. According to Quintilian,

Effects of extraordinary sublimity are produced when the theme is exalted by a bold and almost hazardous metaphor and inanimate objects are given life and action, as in the phrase "Araxes' flood that scorns a bridge."[9]

In a passage often cited by eighteenth-century critics,[10] Longinus praised Homer's personification of Strife or Discord in the *Iliad* as an example of the true sublime. The description of Strife, who "rises small at first, but presently/presses her head on heaven and strides the earth," is said by Longinus to be "no less a measure of Homer than of Strife."[11]

If personification occupied a well-established and highly respected place in the literary theory and practice of the ancients, it was prominent also in the works of the better-known English poets. Spenser's numerous personifications and the figures of Sin and Death in *Paradise Lost* testified to the importance of the personified abstraction in English poetry. Early eighteenth-century poets and critics did not lack respectable precedents concerning the ways in which the figure could, or should, be used.

In the early eighteenth century, as E. N. Hooker notes, "there was evidently a strong taste for instruction in the form of allegory." All critics, so far as Hooker is able to discover, "agreed upon the necessity for allegory [in the epic poem], though there were a few who protested against the practice of reading allegory everywhere in the epic."[12] What critics have to say about a particular figure of speech is incidental to their broader interests. Since everyone was interested in the epic, and since the allegorical interpretation figures so largely in epic criticism, an examination of this criticism will provide the best point of departure for an investigation of early eighteenth-century attitudes toward the personified abstraction.

The critical opinions of John Dennis and Joseph Addison have been chosen for review in this connection because the comparison reveals the difference between earlier traditional attitudes and those newer attitudes toward the personified abstraction which derive largely from the application to literary criticism of the principles of English empirical philosophy, as formulated especially in the writings of John Locke.

John Dennis made allegory a cardinal point in his theory of the epic. The fable of an epic poem, according to Dennis, "is the Imitation of an Action; that is, it is an Universal and Allegorical Action."[13] What Dennis says here is only what everyone admitted, namely, that the epic should have a moral and that the moral lesson should be of universal validity.[14] It was by no means necessary to allegorize everything in Homer and Virgil in order to substantiate such a view: one might find a "universal" moral in the anger of Achilles or in the piety of Aeneas without regarding the gods or other personages as embodiments of a particular moral quality. It appears, however, that Dennis regards every "machine" in the epic as endowed with allegorical significance. "The antient Poets," he writes approvingly, "made their *Machines* allegorical, as well as their human Persons."[15] This statement appears in Dennis's attack on the *Rape of the Lock*. Dennis criticizes Pope's *Rape* as if it were a true epic, but like most critics of the late seventeenth century he pays little attention to the lesser poetic "kinds." So far as nondramatic poetry is concerned, Dennis is interested chiefly in the epic and in the ode, the two "kinds" comprising the "higher" poetry. Regardless of the type of poem he is discussing, he tends to view it as approaching one or the other of these forms and criticizes it accordingly.

An allegorical meaning is essential to the epic—including the mock-epic—because every epic has a fable, and "there cannot possibly be any Fable, that is, any Action founded upon a Moral, but what is allegorical."[16] One is entitled to infer from this that Dennis does not regard the personified abstractions which appear in epic poetry as figures of fancy, intended to appeal to the imagination rather than to the "understanding." Each of them has allegorical significance, and for the critic this is the most important fact about them. The emphasis in Dennis's criticism is always on the didactic value of the abstraction. The possible esthetic value of the abstraction as a poetic image tends to be ignored, or to be regarded as a secondary characteristic not worthy of serious critical attention.

Dennis's attitude, for instance, toward Virgil's figure of Fame in the *Aeneid* is traditional in the sense that he makes no distinction between the goddess Fame and the other deities that figure in the poem. Such an attitude is natural enough since it was well known that the ancients regarded such figures as deities and worshipped them in their temples. Dennis, accordingly, does not distinguish any quality peculiar to Fame as an abstraction which she does not possess as an allegorical "machine," and the significance of such machines lay in their appeal to the rational faculty. They were of interest because of the particular moral they exemplified.

Virgil, says Dennis, "describes his Machines succinctly, if he describes them at all; and rather chooses to say what they do than what they are." He admits that the figure of Fame "is drawn in fifteen Lines at length; three of which Number describe her Person," but justifies this lengthy description by the importance of Fame in the plot context: she is said to cause the departure of Aeneas and the death of Dido.[17] Dennis says, indeed, that "there can be no Poetry without . . . description; that is, without Painting," but the type of description he has in mind is not the delineation of external appearances "but action, clearly and vigorously describ'd."[18] Everything in poetry must have life, because, in order to interest the reader, poetry must excite passion. The reader's emotions must be aroused, and Dennis believes this can be effectively accomplished only in those cases where the poet emphasizes movement or activity, especially where such activity is represented as the result of strong emotion. Emotion depicted in poetry will produce corresponding emotions in the breast of the

reader, but mere description, however pleasing, is not stimulating: it does not excite passion.

On occasion, however, the description of outward appearances
may approach the sublime. This happens not when the poet has
endeavored to describe fully but when he has deliberately left
something to the imagination of the reader. Dennis praises Virgil's description of Venus because only her hair and the back of
her neck are mentioned. "A Poet," he says,

without Judgment, would certainly have describ'd her Face. But
Virgil has discernment enough to see, that what he had said of her
Hair, and of her Neck, and her Mien, would set her Face before the
Reader in a more ravishing Form, than all the most beautiful Colours
in Poetry, and the most delicate exquisite Strokes of the greatest of
masters could paint it.[19]

Dennis, says Hooker,

believed that the force of poetic suggestion, which impelled the imagination to build upon the merest hints, was the chief sign of the
Sublime.[20]

There is little place, then, in Dennis's critical theory for the
lavishly detailed abstraction, or for any prosopopoeia which is intended to appeal solely to one's sense of the beautiful. He is not
interested in such figures unless they are seen to evoke a powerful emotional appeal as instances of the imaginative sublime or
are seen to play a significant role in the narrative structure of the
poem as epic "machines." Dennis

thought of literary allegory as a means of asserting an ethical proposition by means of unified plot or action, or of demonstrating the
social or moral value of certain universal traits by embodying them
in specific characters.

He would not have appreciated Spenserian allegory. because he
lacked the virtue displayed by John Hughes "who recognized
that supernatural and allegorical creatures were justified in poetry
if they are 'amusing to the Imagination.' "[21]

Addison's papers on the pleasures of the imagination in the *Spectator* represent a new departure in literary criticism. C. D. Thorpe maintains that Addison's original intention was to discuss only the primary pleasures of the imagination, that is, those which "occur in the presence of beautiful or great or novel objects in nature, or of works of architecture." The papers on the secondary pleasures aroused by literature and by the representative arts are accounted for by Thorpe as a result of Addison's interest, which grew upon him as he worked, "in adapting the principles of imaginative response to literary criticism."[22] Addison's chief contribution to critical theory lies in this adaptation. His theories concerning the nature of the imagination itself, and of the way it functions, are not original; they are derived from contemporary empirical thought, as formulated in the writings of John Locke. As a "Lockian and an empiricist," Addison adopts

the introspective method of the new philosophy. He proposes to look into the mind to find there what objects please, how they please, and why. He will analyze both the causes and the effects of the pleasures in question, and from this analysis will attempt to deduce new principles by which to judge art, in place of the then prevailing Rules of neo-classic criticism.[23]

Like Dennis, Addison stressed the allegorical significance of personified abstractions. His own prose allegories, as E. R. Wasserman says, reflect the popularity of the abstraction as a pleasing device for inculcating morality.[24] But Addison recognized, as Hughes did, that allegorical figures were justified if they were "amusing" to the imagination. "The Pleasures of the Imagination," he wrote,

are often to be met with among the Polite Masters of Morality, Criticism, and other Speculations abstracted from Matter, who, tho' they do not directly treat of the visible Parts of Nature, often draw from them their Similitudes, Metaphors and Allegories. By these Allusions a Truth in the Understanding is as it were reflected by the Imagination; we are able to see something like Colour and Shape in a Notion, and to discover a Scheme of Thoughts traced out upon

Matter. And here the Mind receives a great deal of Satisfaction, and has two of its Faculties gratified at the same time, while the Fancie is busie in copying after the Understanding, and transcribing Ideas out of the Intellectual World into the Material.

"Allegories," in consequence, "are like so many Tracks of Light in a Discourse, that make every thing about them clear and beautiful." The personified abstraction appeals to the imagination by its "Colour and Shape," and "it is this Talent of affecting the Imagination, that gives an Embellishment to good Sense, and makes one Man's Compositions more agreeable than another's."[25] The pleasure we take in allegory, as in other types of imagery, is the result of a faculty of mind which operates automatically:

It is but opening the Eye, and the Scene enters. The Colours paint themselves on the Fancy, with very little Attention of Thought or Application of Mind in the Beholder. We are struck, we know not how, with the Symmetry of any thing we see, and immediately assent to the Beauty of an Object, without enquiring into the particular Causes and Occasions of it.[26]

Addison is speaking of the primary pleasures of the imagination rather than of the secondary, or literary, pleasures; but, as his preceding remarks show, he makes no significant distinction between the two:

A beautiful Prospect delights the Soul, as much as a Demonstration; and a Description in *Homer* has charm'd more Readers than a Chapter in *Aristotle*.[27]

The imagination reacts in the same way to the poetic description of agreeable objects as it does when the objects are present to the eye of the beholder.

The imagination is not a purely passive faculty, engaged simply in registering and automatically reacting to external stimuli. For Addison the pleasures of the imagination, "taken in the full Extent, are not so gross as those of Sense, nor so refined as those of the Understanding."[28] Pleasure is received from some impres-

sions, not from others. An act of discrimination is necessarily involved, even though this represents a spontaneous reaction rather
than a conscious exercise of the critical reason. It is this element
of judgment, acting spontaneously, which serves to place the
imagination at one remove from sense perception (in which
judgment is not a factor) and the understanding faculty, in
which the critical reason operates consciously.

Having made his decision to relate the principles of imaginative response to literary criticism, Addison is led to make a systematic survey of those objects in poetry which are found to
please. In addition to objects which exist in nature, the poets frequently describe phenomena which have no existence in the
world of empirical reality. It is in the course of his discussion of
these "fictions" that Addison is led to distinguish the personified
abstraction as a literary device distinct from other types of imagery, not because of its particular function in any one poem, but
because of the peculiar qualities which attach to it as a "fiction."
In *Spectator* 419 he associates the allegorical abstraction with the
"Fairy Way of Writing." The same "particular Cast of Fancy"
which is responsible for the production of "Fairies, Witches and
the like Imaginary Persons" is operative also when the poet "represents any Passion, Appetite, Virtue or Vice, under a visible
Shape, and makes it a Person or an Actor in his Poem."[29] This
fairy way of writing

is, indeed, more difficult than any other that depends on the Poet's
Fancy, because he has no Pattern to follow in it, and must work altogether out of his own Invention.[30]

Addison thought it showed "a greater Genius in *Shakespear* to
have drawn his *Calyban,* than his *Hotspur* or *Julius Caesar"* because

the one was to be supplied out of his own Imagination, whereas
the other might have been formed upon Tradition, History and Observation.[31]

John Dennis considers the personified abstraction as it appears

in the epic and finds it a part of the usual epic machinery. Convinced that the real importance of epic machines lies in the moral
they exemplify, Dennis does not distinguish critically between
abstractions as such and the gods and goddesses of the classical
pantheon. For Addison, however, the most important fact about
the allegorical abstraction is not the function it has in the poem
but the fact that it is "fiction," and therefore differs in kind from
poetic fabrications based upon prototypes to be found in nature.
Addison was fully aware of the fact that "Allegorical Persons"
were worshipped as deities by the "Heathens," but the fact that
"we now regard such a Person as entirely shadowy and unsub-
stantial" appeared sufficient reason for distinguishing between
the abstraction as such and the other deities of the classical pantheon.[32]

Emphasizing the "fictional" character of personified abstractions as the quality which sets them apart from other products of
the poet's invention, Addison does not think "that Persons of
such a chymerical Existence are Proper Actors in an Epic Poem;
because there is not that Measure of Probability annexed to them,
which is requisite in Writings of this Kind."[33] Virgil's description of the goddess Fame might be excused on the ground that
"the Part she acts is very short,"[34] but the same could not be said
of Milton's figures of Sin and Death. These, accordingly, are condemned for the part they play in the action of the poem, although
they are praised for their intrinsic sublimity.[35] The persistent
strength of the feeling which prompts Addison's criticism is evident in eighteenth-century comment on the Sin-Death episode. A
few critics praise Milton's figures unreservedly;[36] most, however,
share Addison's views on the impropriety of these abstractions as
"actors" in an epic poem.[37]

Not all personified abstractions were straightforwardly allegorical. Some of them were "just shewn without being engaged
in any Series of Action." Figures of this sort were to be regarded
as "Poetical Phrases" rather than as "Allegorical Descriptions."
They were simply "short Expressions, which convey an ordinary

Thought to the Mind in the most pleasing Manner." Thus Homer, "instead of telling us that Men naturally fly when they are terrified . . . introduces the Persons of *Flight* and *Fear,* who, he tells us, are inseparable Companions." Addison believed himself the first to have treated of personified abstractions which were "just shewn without being engaged in any Series of Action."[38] However this may be, Addison is certainly the first critic to deal with them systematically as a group.

Personifications of whatever type were sometimes to be regarded as products of the very highest levels of imaginative exertion. Thus, "the descriptive Part" of Milton's allegory of Sin and Death is said to be "full of sublime Ideas":

> The figure of Death, the Regal Crown upon his Head, his Menace to Satan, his advancing to the Combat, the Outcry at his Birth, are Circumstances too noble to be past over in Silence, and extremely suitable to this *King of Terrors.*[39]

As one might expect, the Bible is considered a veritable repository of "sublime Ideas." The following passage sheds light on Addison's theory of the sublime. "I do not know," he says,

> any imaginary Person made use of in a more sublime manner of Thinking than that in one of the Prophets, who describing God as descending from Heaven, and visiting the Sins of Mankind, adds that dreadful Circumstance, *Before him went the Pestilence.* It is certain this imaginary Person might have been described in all her purple Spots. The Fever might have marched before her, Pain might have stood at her Right Hand, Phrenzy on her Left, and Death in her Rear. . . . But I believe every Reader will think, that in such sublime Writings the mentioning of her as it is done in Scripture, has something in it more just, as well as great, than all that the most fanciful Poet could have bestowed upon her in the Richness of his Imagination.[40]

Addison's view of the sublime is similar to that of Dennis. It is the force of suggestion, "which impels the imagination to build upon the merest hints," that constitutes the chief sign of the sublime.

Whether "sublime" or merely "pleasing," all types of personified abstractions were to be classified as poetic "fictions." As such,
they acquired the prestige which eighteenth-century critics gave
to "original" invention. As Thomas Parnell said,

> There seems to be no likelier way by which a poetical genius may
> yet appear as an original, than that he should proceed with a full
> compass of thought and knowledge, either to design his plan, or
> to beautify the parts of it, in an allegorical manner.[41]

John Hughes, whose *Essay on Allegorical Poetry* shows the influence of Addison, emphasizes the "wild" and fictitious nature
of personified abstractions. Like Addison, Hughes associates the
abstraction with fairies and other beings which are "out of Nature":

> An Allegory sometimes, for the sake of the moral Sense couch'd
> under its Fictions, gives Speech to Brutes, and sometimes intro-
> duces Creatures which are out of Nature, as Goblins, Chimaera's,
> Fairies, and the like; so it frequently gives Life to Virtues and Vices,
> Passions and Diseases, to natural and moral Qualities; and represents
> them acting as divine, human, or infernal Persons.[42]

That kind of allegory, says Hughes, which may

> properly challenge the Name, is that in which the Fable or Story con-
> sists for the most part of fictitious Persons or Beings, Creatures of
> the Poet's Brain, and Actions surprising, and without the Bounds of
> Probability or Nature. In Works of this kind, it is impossible for
> the Reader to rest in the literal Sense, but he is of necessity driven to
> seek for another Meaning under these wild Types and Shadows.[43]

A particular state of mind was often felt to be necessary for the
fabrication of such imaginary persons. Addison usually describes
his prose allegories as the products of dream or trance. He apolo-
gizes for one of them on the ground that "the wildness of imagination, which in a dream is always loose and irregular, discovers
itself too much in several parts of it."[44] As Wasserman notes, the
state of mind which results in the production of personifications
was generally assumed to be one of vehement feelings. Personifi-

cations were thought to result from "flights" of imagination, and it was assumed that such flights would most naturally occur when the rational mind was laid to sleep as in dreams or visions.[45] "Vision or apostrophe," said a critic writing in the latter half of the century, "is the imaginary presence of absent beings, and predominates in all its excess, in the intervals of reason, as in the case of dreaming or madness."[46]

It should be emphasized, however, that the qualities of "wildness" and "irregularity" were associated with the act of mind responsible for the conception of beings "out of nature" rather than with the particular form or function assumed by such beings in the poem itself. Paradoxical as it may seem, it was the eighteenth-century bias in favor of the "natural" as opposed to the "unnatural" which was largely responsible for the prestige accorded the poet who was successful in the fabrication of beings "out of nature." A poem was an imitation of nature, and while the imitative theory did not necessarily imply that the poet should confine himself to the data of empirical reality, the tendency to interpret the theory literally was always present, and is one reason for the critical interest in poetic fabrications which had no obvious prototypes in the real world. It was not so much a question of the way in which the poet should write, as of the way in which he was compelled to write. It was "natural" for the poet to model his images upon examples met with in nature or upon those found in other writers. The creation of images which had no prototypes in the real world appeared difficult because the poet had seemingly ignored the aids which the great majority of poets had always used, or were popularly supposed to have used. If successful, the poet was admired almost as much for his skill in overcoming the difficulties supposedly inherent in this type of imaginative creation as for the poetic effectiveness of the images themselves. The successful image of this type was not necessarily expected to exhibit, either in form or in function, any of the extravagancies suggested by the terms "wildness" and "irregularity." Addison anticipates the judgment of later critics when he praises Shakespeare's "Fairies, Witches and the like Imaginary Persons" because "we cannot forbear thinking them natural, tho' we have no Rule by which to judge of them, and must confess, if there are such Beings in the World, it looks highly probable they should talk and act as he has represented them."[47] The eighteenth century reserved a high measure of admiration for the poet who was able to incorporate the fabrications of fantasy into the natural world. The triumph of imagination lay in the creation of beings which, although "unreal," were made to impress the reader with their entire truth to nature. Hence, the creations of the "wildest" imagination must always be "just"; that is, they must be found to satisfy contemporary demands for propriety, clarity of presentation, and the other requisites of neoclassic literary criticism.

The use of "fiction" as a means of inculcating the truths of morality was a cause of uneasiness to some. Edward Bysshe exhibits the contemporary distrust of fiction *per se* when he finds it necessary to defend his translations of "Descriptions merely fabulous" on the ground that "the well-invented Fables of the Antients were design'd only to inculcate the Truth with more Delight, and to make it shine with greater Splendour."[48] Indeed, the ultimate justification for allegory lay not in the evidence of its utility but in the opinion of its necessity. In the last analysis, a defense of allegory on the ground of its moral utility alone was felt to be inadequate. It was all too evident that moral truths could be more fully and more adequately expressed in unadorned prose. The justification for allegory had to cut deeper; it tends to be based, ultimately, upon the nature of man himself as revealed through the teachings of Christianity. We are "averse" to "Precepts of morality," said Addison, because of the "natural corruption of our tempers."[49] "Truth," said Henry Felton,

is ever most beautiful, and evident in her native Dress: And the Arts that are used to convey her to our Minds, are no Argument that she is deficient, but so many Testimonies of the Corruption of our Nature, when Truth, of all Things the plainest and sincerest, is forced to gain Admittance to us in Disguise, and court us in Masquerade.[50]

Allegories, therefore, "are not so much any Ornament of Style, as an artful Way of recommending Truth to the World in a borrowed Shape, and a Dress more agreeable to the Fancy, than naked Truth herself can be."[51] Allegory tends to be regarded as a necessary form of sugar-coating for the pill of moral instruction. Such an interpretation enhances the prestige of allegorical figures as important elements in a way of writing which is thought to derive its sanction from one of the fundamental characteristics of human nature.

The contribution of Addison toward a theory of personification may now be summarized as follows. He associates the personified abstraction with the imagination as opposed to the understanding. He calls attention to the existence of the figure as a device more remarkable for its inherent than for its accidental qualities. He considers the figure as the product of both the lower and higher levels of imaginative exertion. At the lower level the prosopopoeia becomes "a short Expression" which conveys "particular Circumstances to the Reader after an unusual and entertaining Manner." At the higher level it becomes an instance of the imaginative sublime. But even where this cannot be said, the use of the figure very often presupposes a measure of strong feeling on the part of the poet and an imagination momentarily released from the restraints imposed by reason. The figure is associated with poetic "fiction" as opposed to prosaic "truth," with the unreal as opposed to the real. Addison praises the fairy way of writing because, in the creation of "Imaginary Persons," the poet "has no Pattern to follow . . . and must work altogether out of his own Invention."

But how is it possible, one may well ask at this point, for the poet to create fabrications not based upon "Tradition, History and Observation?" As a good empiricist, Addison emphasizes visible objects as the raw material from which the imagination forms its creations. He is at pains to define his philosophical position in the very first number of the series of papers on the pleasures of imagination. By these, he means only such pleasures "as arise originally from Sight." The imagination receives all its materials from external nature through the visual sense, so that "we cannot . . . have a single Image in the Fancy that did not make its first Entrance through the Sight," although, once these materials are received, the imagination is able to retain, alter, and compound them

> into all the Varieties of Picture and Vision that are most agreeable to the Imagination; for by this Faculty a Man in a Dungeon is capable of entertaining himself with Scenes and Landskips more beautiful than any that can be found in the whole Compass of Nature.[52]

How, then, can the poet be said to work "altogether out of his own Invention?" However altered or "compounded," the materials which go into the making of the poetic image are to be traced, ultimately, to impressions of sight. The image need not be based upon tradition or history, but Addison appears to contradict himself when he says that it need not be based upon "Observation." I am not concerned here with any attempt at resolving this apparent inconsistency. Addison might have replied that since the "compound" image represents a new whole it is not based upon observation in the same sense as those images which have their counterparts in nature. One should, I believe, regard Addison's remarks on the fairy way of writing as intended to emphasize the difference between this and other ways of writing rather than as the expression of a reasoned belief in the imagination as a faculty capable of forming images owing nothing whatsoever to "Tradition, History and Observation." But whether or not Addison believed the imagination capable in some instances of fabricating images not based ultimately upon sense impressions, the emphasis on objects of sight as the customary materials from which the imagination draws its images explains the degree of admiration which Addison gives to those poets successful in the fabrication of beings "out of nature." His

admiration is based upon the old principle of "difficulty overcome."[53]

This may be the place to explain my use of the term "empirical." I use the word in referring to certain aspects of the Lockian
philosophy which I find to be of considerable importance in
the formation of what has been called "the mechanical theory of
literary invention."[54] I do not mean to deny the importance of
the "rationalist" element in eighteenth-century philosophy. "Empirical" as used in this book is simply a general descriptive term
for philosophies which purport to derive all knowledge, or the
greater part of it, from impressions of sense as distinguished
(typically) from philosophies which, like that of Descartes, ad-
mit the possibility of "innate ideas."

Hobbes himself states the fundamental premise of eighteenth-
century empirical philosophy when he says that the thoughts of
man have an "Originall," and that this original "is that which
we call SENSE," for "there is no conception in a man's mind,
which hath not at first, totally, or by parts, been begotten upon
the organs of *Sense*."[55] In the famous passage on decaying sense,
Hobbes limits the term "imagination" to mean the after-recollec-
tion of visible objects. The "Latines," he maintains, applied the
word "improperly" to include impressions received from the
other senses, when it should signify only "the image made in
seeing." There are two sorts of imagination, the *"simple"* and
the "Compounded"; the former

is the imagining the whole object, as it was presented to the sense
. . . as when one imagineth a man, or horse, which he hath seen
before. The other is *Compounded;* as when from the sight of a man
at one time, and of a horse at another, we conceive in our mind a
Centaure. So when a man compoundeth the image of his own person,
with the image of the actions of an other man; as when a man im-
agins himselfe a *Hercules,* or an *Alexander,* (which happeneth often
to them that are much taken with reading of Romants) it is a compound imagination, and properly but a Fiction of the mind.[56]

With the exception of those few critics who still retain a belief in the existence of innate ideas, this theory of imagination remains virtually unchallenged for nearly one hundred and fifty years. Eighteenth-century philosophers and critics may and do refine upon it, but they do not replace it with something "new." They fill in the details, but they do not alter the basic structure. "Simple ideas," said Locke, are "the materials of all our knowledge":

When the understanding is once stored with these simple ideas, it has the power to repeat, compare, and unite them, even to an almost infinite variety, and so can make at pleasure new complex ideas. But it is not in the power of the most exalted wit, or enlarged understanding, by any quickness or variety of thought, to *invent* or *frame* one new simple idea in the mind . . . [which a man has not] received in by his senses from external objects, or by reflection from the operations of his own mind about them.[57]

Hobbes, Locke, and Addison agree in denying the possibility of any transcendental source for the materials employed in the operations of imagination. Nor is there any quality in the imagination itself which is able to form images or ideas[58] not derived from impressions of sense.

Peter Browne's book on the human understanding may be taken as representative of the way in which Locke's ideas were understood in the early eighteenth century. Browne emphasizes the sense basis upon which all knowledge rests:

I shall premise it as a sure and uncontested Truth; That we have no other *Faculties* of perceiving or knowing any thing divine or human but our *Five Senses,* and our *Reason.* The Contexture of our Frame is so various and complicated, that it is no easy matter nicely to distinguish our understanding Faculties from one another; and Men who would appear more sharp-sighted than others, and pry farther into this matter than there is occasion, may increase the number of those Faculties: But they will be all comprehended under *Sense,* by which the Ideas of external sensible Objects are first conveyed into the *Imagination;* and *Reason* or the pure Intellect, which operates upon those Ideas, and upon them, *Only* after they are so lodged in that common Receptacle.[59]

Later and more eminent eighteenth-century philosophers and men of letters agreed with Browne. Edmund Burke observes that

the mind of man possesses a sort of creative power of its own; either in representing at pleasure the images of things in the order and manner in which they were received by the senses, or in combining those images in a new manner, and according to a different order. This power is called imagination; and to this belongs whatever is called wit, fancy, invention, and the like. But it must be observed, that this power of the imagination is incapable of producing anything absolutely new; it can only vary the disposition of those ideas which it has received from the senses.[60]

David Hume also recognizes the creative power which imagination has, but, he adds,

though our thought seems to possess this unbounded liberty, we shall find, upon a nearer examination, that it is really confined within very narrow limits, and that all this creative power of the mind amounts to no more than the faculty of compounding, transposing, augmenting, or diminishing the materials afforded by us by the senses and experience. When we think of a golden mountain, we only join two consistent ideas, *gold,* and *mountain,* with which we were formerly acquainted. A virtuous horse we can conceive; because, from our own feeling, we can conceive virtue; and this we may unite to the figure and shape of a horse, which is an animal familiar to us.[61]

J. H. Hagstrum calls this statement by Hume "an excellent summary of the basic theory to which Johnson adhered."[62] Johnson once

expressed the opinion that the poetry of St. Kilda must be very poor because the locality was barren of images and therefore starved the poet's fancy. To Boswell's objection that even what material there was could be combined into poetry by "a poetical genius," Johnson replied: "But, sir, a man cannot make fire but in proportion as he has wood. He cannot coin guineas but in proportion as he has gold."[63]

"Imagination," said Johnson, "is useless without knowledge: nature gives in vain the power of combination, unless study and observation supply materials to be combined."[64] One notes, incidentally, that John Locke is "pre-eminently" the philosopher of Johnson's *Dictionary,* "one of its most important prose sources."[65] It would not be difficult to collect passages from Johnson's writings which would seem to imply a belief in a power of mind which is able to form conceptions not based upon "Tradition, History and Observation." He defines "fantastical," for instance, as "Irrational; bred only in the imagination."[66] But this is the expression of an emotional attitude rather than a statement of philosophic principle. Johnson slips into such language when expressing his fear of imaginative indulgence carried to excess; Addison, one notes, invokes similar language to express his emotional response to those "fictions" of imagination (e.g., Caliban) which meet with his enthusiastic approval.

The student of eighteenth-century criticism will frequently encounter glowing praises of various authors for their "originality" and "invention." Such authors will be said to have formed conceptions and images entirely new and completely foreign to all mere sensory experience. It is important to remember that such conceptions were thought of as "new" only in the sense attributed to Homer's Chimera by Alexander Gerard. When Homer formed the idea of his Chimera, said Gerard, he did not create anything new, for "the brightest imagination can suggest no idea which is not originally derived from sense and memory." Homer only joined into one animal the different parts of others.[67] We are able to imagine forms which have no archetype in nature because the

IMAGINATION is first of all employed in presenting such ideas, as are not attended with *remembrance,* or a perception of their having been formerly in the mind. This defect of remembrance, as it prevents our referring them to their original sensations, dissolves their natural connection. But when *memory* has lost their real bonds of union, *fancy,* by its associating power, confers upon them new ties, [and] that they may not lie perfectly loose, ranges them in an endless variety of forms. Many of these being representations of nothing that exists in nature, whatever is fictitious or chimerical is acknowledged to be the offspring of this faculty, and is termed imaginary.[68]

These ideas are "representations of nothing that exists in nature" in so far as they represent new wholes created by the combination of different ideas, but each separate idea is traceable to one original "sensation" or sensory impression of something which has a real existence in external nature. Lord Kames's view of the imagination is similar to that of Addison and Gerard. According to Kames:

Man is endued with a sort of creative power: he can fabricate images of things that have no existence. The materials employ'd in this operation, are ideas of sight, which he can take to pieces and combine into new forms at pleasure: their complexity and vivacity make them fit materials. But a man hath no such power over any of his other ideas, whether of the external or internal senses: he cannot, after the utmost effort, combine these into new forms, being too obscure for that operation. An image thus fabricated cannot be called a secondary perception, not being derived from an original perception: the poverty of language however . . . has occasioned the same term *idea* to be apply'd to all. This singular power of fabricating images without any foundation in reality, is distinguished by the name *imagination*.[69]

Kames's "original perception" is the image we have of an object at the moment of sight. The "secondary perception" is "that perception of a real object which is raised in the mind by the power of memory."[70] There is no qualitative difference between the two:

After attentively surveying a fine statue, I close my eyes. What follows? The same object continues, without any difference but that it is less distinct than formerly. This indistinct secondary perception of an object, is termed an *idea*.[71]

The image formed by the combination of various "ideas" of sight cannot be called a secondary perception since it is itself derived from a number of secondary perceptions, variously combined. Nevertheless, Kames's explanation still carries one back to the original perceptions of sight as the sources from which the "ideas," however "combined," are ultimately derived.

John Aikin emphasizes the "fictional" aspect of imagination. An ardent admirer of the personifications of Spenser, Aikin delights in such imaginative "fictions." The imagination "peoples the world with new beings, it embodies abstract ideas, it suggests unexpected resemblances, it creates first, and then presides over its creation with absolute sway."[72] Nevertheless, these "fictions" could be endowed only with such human qualities "as we see existing among ourselves." All personifications of abstract qualities are based ultimately upon impressions of sense:

Even the external figures of beauty and deformity in our imaginations, must be mere transcripts of pictures already formed by our senses. We can compound differently from what nature has done; we can aggrandize and diminish; but we can form no truly original conceptions.[73]

Dugald Stewart extends the province of imagination to include not objects of sense merely but "all the different subjects of our knowledge":

As it is the same power of Reasoning which enables us to carry on our investigations with respect to individual objects, and with respect to classes or genera; so it was by the same processes of analysis and combination, that the genius of Milton produced the Garden of Eden; that of Harrington, the Commonwealth of Oceana; and that of Shakespeare, the characters of Hamlet and Falstaff. The difference between these several efforts of genius consists only in the manner in which the original materials were acquired: so far as the power of Imagination is concerned, the processes are perfectly analogous.[74]

To Addison, these "several efforts of genius" were understood to be a part of the reasoning faculty, distinguished under the separate headings of judgment, taste, and the like. Stewart considers them, rather, as immediately involved in any act of imaginative creation. The imagination is, accordingly, "a complex power." It includes

Conception or simple Apprehension, which enables us to form a notion of those former objects of perception or of knowledge, out of which we are to make a selection; Abstraction, which separates the selected materials from the qualities and circumstances which are connected with them in nature; and Judgment or Taste, which selects the materials, and directs their combination. To these powers, we may add, that particular habit of association to which I formerly gave the name of Fancy; as it is this which presents to our choice, all the different materials which are subservient to the efforts of Imagination, and which may therefore be considered as forming the groundwork of poetical genius.[75]

Thus, in Milton's account of the Garden of Eden, the "Association of Ideas" suggested to Milton

a variety of the most striking scenes which he had seen . . . and the power of Conception placed each of them before him with all its beauties and imperfections. In every natural scene, if we destine it for any particular purpose, there are defects and redundancies . . . Milton, accordingly, would not copy his Eden from any one scene, but would select from each the features which were most eminently beautiful. The power of Abstraction enabled him to make the separation, and Taste directed him in the selection.[76]

The imagination creates an ideal landscape, but this landscape is not "bred only in the imagination": the materials from which it is formed are abstracted from the world of empirical reality.

It has been said that Stewart

anticipated (and perhaps influenced) Coleridge in distinguishing between the imagination and the fancy—the fancy, according to Stewart, constituting a lower faculty that proffers sensible materials upon which the imagination operates by its complex powers of "apprehension," "abstraction," and "taste."[77]

The terms "fancy" and "imagination" are synonymous for most eighteenth-century critics, but it is true that as the century proceeds imagination comes to be looked upon by some as the higher degree of a power of which fancy represents the lower degree. Mrs. Piozzi, for instance, does not find the two terms "wholly synonymous":

We . . . say, that Milton has displayed a boundless IMAGINATION in his poem of Paradise Lost—transporting us as it were into the very depths of eternity, while he describes the journey of Satan and the games of the fallen angels; but that Pope's Rape of the Lock is a work of exquisite FANCY, almost emulative of Shakespeare's creative powers—not servilely imitating him.[78]

It seems clear, however, that both terms still refer to the power of mind which creates "unreal" scenes of being. There is no evidence that late eighteenth-century critics differ from their predecessors in their views concerning the essential nature of the creative process itself. Although "Coleridge himself was indebted to English precedent for some of his leading ideas," it is true, nevertheless, that

Coleridge's theory of mind, like that of contemporary German philosophers, was, as he insisted, revolutionary; it was, in fact, part of a change in the habitual way of thinking, in all areas of intellectual enterprise, which is as sharp and dramatic as any the history of ideas can show.[79]

Stewart's analysis of the distinction between "fancy" and "imagination" does not involve an approach to an "organic" theory of imagination such as that held by Coleridge. His analysis of the poetic imagination "follows the eighteenth-century pattern." The creative power of imagination

consists only in the fact that it is able "to make a selection of qualities and of circumstances, from a variety of different objects, and by combining and disposing these to form a new creation of its own."[80]

The period of time which separates Hobbes's Leviathan (1651) from Stewart's Elements of the Philosophy of the Human Mind (1792) does not seem so very long. Addison's "dungeon" scene, Gerard's Chimera, Hume's golden mountain, and Stewart's Miltonic landscape are all fabrications of that same "compound imagination" which produced Hobbes's Centaure. Other elements have been added to the basic conception, the extreme complexity of the mental process involved has become more or less apparent, but the main features of the design survive unaltered.

Hobbes, it will be noted, does not regard the simple image as so much a "fiction" as the compound image. The simple image may be referred to its prototype in nature; it is so far "real." The compound image, on the other hand, has no prototype in nature; it is consequently much more a "Fiction of the mind." The image of a centaur appeared more of a fiction than an image of Alexander or Hercules. Alexander had once a real existence in nature, and Hercules, whether real in this sense or not, was more real than any fiction of a centaur since the appropriate image could be derived from the observation of one's "own person." A figure then, such as Caliban, was more evidently a fiction of the mind than Shakespeare's Lear, for Caliban, unlike Lear, had no living archetype in the material world. Caliban, as Dryden puts it, is "a species of himself, begotten by an incubus on a witch." Dryden wishes to show that Shakespeare's "boldness" in creating Caliban was not altogether "intolerable"; he attempts to take off from the unfamiliarity which such a figure had for his readers by noting that, just as "from the distinct apprehensions of a horse, and of a man, imagination has formed a centaur; so from those of an incubus and a sorceress, Shakespeare has produced his monster."[81] Traditional articles of popular belief would provide the materials for the separate conceptions of incubus and sorceress; Dryden can then proceed to show that the process of mind which gives rise to Caliban is not itself unfamiliar, or in any way peculiar. Caliban, like the centaur of the ancients, is a product of the "compound" imagination.

"Is not Lear as much a fiction as Caliban?" asks D. G. James in commenting upon the implications of Hobbes's theory of imagination.[82] Our answer must be in the negative so far as the eighteenth century is concerned. Lear is not so much a fiction as Caliban, and by a like process of reasoning the personified abstraction becomes, not indeed so much a fiction as Caliban, but considerably more of a fiction than Lear. The personified abstraction had its prototype in nature so far as it required the attribution of specific human traits, but the abstract quality itself had no such prototype in the world of material reality. The poet who personified could not draw upon the living representations which formed the raw material, so to speak, out of which Shakespeare created his Lear. It is this kind of reasoning which is responsible for Addison's inclusion of the personified abstraction in the list of those creatures which appear in the fairy way of writing.

The prestige, then, which the personified abstraction may have in the eighteenth century will depend to a considerable extent upon the attitude of poets and their readers toward "fictions of the mind" as material for poetry in contrast to the poetic delineation of objects, persons, or scenes of being which could be said to have a real existence in external nature. I attempt in this book to reach some conclusions in regard to the strength of the sentiment in favor of such "fictions" as material for poetry, and I try to determine what effect this sentiment had upon the use of the personified abstraction in eighteenth-century verse. One should remember, in this connection, that the fabrication of these compound images or "fictions" was associated with the creative power of mind. Although unable to create anything absolutely "new," the poet who was successful in the fabrication of praeternatural beings, whether monsters, personified abstractions, or other beings "out of nature," was a poet of "original" invention; he created first, and then presided over his creation "with absolute sway."

But the personified abstraction was not only a "fiction"; it was a "sensible" image. To gain an adequate understanding of its position in eighteenth-century poetics, one must consider the formal characteristics which it was expected to exhibit. The next chapter begins, therefore, with a discussion of the prosopopoeia as an "object of sight."

CHAPTER II

THE PERSONIFIED ABSTRACTION AS
A "FICTION OF THE MIND"

"WE CAN SAFELY SAY," writes C. D. Thorpe, "that, so far as we find it described in its purer form, imaginative pleasure with Addison is basically related to the picture-making function of mind,"[1] and the imagination itself is regarded "primarily as a picture-receiving, picture-retaining, picture-building faculty, inseparably related to aesthetic response."[2] If, as Addison maintained, the essential distinction between poetry and prose lay in the fact that the former appealed to the imagination and the latter to the understanding, it followed that the poet should be lavish in the description of visible objects since the pleasures of imagination are derived from objects of sight. The images of the poet, therefore, should become "pictures" endowed with "Colour and Shape." As Henry Pemberton said,

If the historian describe a river, a mountain, or a country, he ought to mention chiefly those circumstances, which may make, what he has afterwards to say of them, understood; but the poet must draw a picture of the thing by an enumeration of such particulars, as would strike the eye or other senses of a person present. In giving such images or pictures, the great art of poetic description consists.[3]

The outcome of such views reveals itself in the tendency to equate the imagination or fancy with the picture-making faculty of mind and to regard the imagery which results as constituting the very essence of poetry. "Beautiful descriptions and images," said Addison, "are the spirit and life of Poetry."[4] It is "Beauty of Colouring," said Edward Bysshe, "in which the Poet's Art chiefly consists,"[5] and to Bezaleel Morrice description was "the very essential *Beauty* of *Poetry,* by which, if well-managed, it charms us more, than it seems capable of any other Way."[6]

To endow the abstract with "Colour and Shape" rendered it amenable to the purposes of poetry since "Writers in Poetry and Fiction borrow their several Materials from outward Objects."[7] We have, then, the feeling that descriptive effects should constitute a major concern of the poet. This feeling was greatly enhanced by the tendency to evaluate poetic imagery in terms of the poetry-painting parallel. Underlying this conception of the affinity between the two arts of poetry and painting was the prevailing conception of all art as an imitation of nature. Though the means were various, all the representative arts had this end in common and might be compared with a view to their relative success in attaining the common goal. The painter, said Sir Joshua Reynolds, seeks

to impress the Spectator with the same interest at the sight of his representation, as the Poet has contrived to impress on the Reader by his description: the end is the same in both cases, though the means are and must be different.[8]

The comparison between poetry and painting was especially easy to make because of the formal correspondences which were thought to exist between these two "sister arts." It was commonly felt that "design equals plot" and that "color equals words."[9] Addison, in a celebrated passage, had applied the pictorial test to metaphor. Let the reader suppose, he says, "Metaphors or Images actually painted," for "by this . . . Rule, a Reader may be able to judge of the Union of all Metaphors whatsoever, and determine which are Homogeneous, and which Heterogeneous; or to speak more plainly, which are Consistent and which Inconsistent."[10] William Whitehead thought that images such as allegories, metaphors, and similes should always conform to Addison's test; indeed, to Whitehead, the "pencil" was the proper test of every "piece of poetry" whatsoever.[11]

As might be expected, the tendency to look for what have been called "the obvious characteristics of visual art"[12] in poetic images is especially pronounced among painters or among those interested in art. Jonathan Richardson tried to imagine one of Milton's ruined angels as it would appear on canvas, exclaiming, "O that he [Milton] had painted! and as he Conceiv'd!"[13] A list of Milton's "pictures" is appended to the *Explanatory Notes and Remarks on Milton's Paradise Lost,* together with a commentary pointing out the pictorial qualities to which the reader should respond. Since "but Few have Pencils to Copy [Milton's] Images in their Own Minds,"[14] the two Richardsons endeavor to assist such people in forming "a Well-Chosen Collection of Poetical Pictures."[15] Such pictures, says the elder Richardson in another place, "will finely employ every vacant moment of ones time."[16] John Opie, "who painted at least one scene from the *Faerie Queene,* was reported to be very fond of Spenser because 'No author furnishes so many pictures.' "[17] George Turnbull, the author of a *Treatise on Ancient Painting,* was another who emphasized the pictorial quality of the poetic image: There is no other way, says Turnbull, "of trying the Propriety, Force and Beauty of a poetical Image, but by considering the Picture it forms in the Imagination, as a Picture."[18]

The impulse toward pictorialization resulted occasionally in the attempt to transfer the mental picture to canvas. In her poem *Conversation,* Hannah More wrote:

> What is this power . . .
> This charm, this witchcraft? 'tis attention:
> Mute angel, yes; thy looks dispense
> The silence of intelligence;
> Thy graceful form I well discern,
> In act to listen and to learn.[19]

These lines, said W. W. Pepys, "are beyond all praise, and form such a picture . . . that as soon as I see Mrs. Walsingham, I shall request of her to paint Attention from your beautiful design."[20] There were others who confined themselves to speculation concerning the manner in which personified abstractions might be represented on canvas. The thirteenth stanza of Gray's *Elegy* suggested to the imagination of John Scott an allegorical painting on the grand scale:

Two of Gray's Fore-fathers of the hamlet, might be introduced reposing from their labour; dignity and grace might be given to their forms; the eye of one beaming celestial fire, might cast a regretful look at Knowledge turning from him her folded roll; the other might indignantly regard Penury, who at a distance should, with a calm severity of countenance, point out to him a plough, or some other instrument of that cultivation which it was his lot to attend to.[21]

E. R. Wasserman finds that the majority of eighteenth-century critics urge the necessity of pictorializing abstractions vividly.[22] There was some question, however, concerning the amount of detail which was thought to be most effective in promoting the vivid mental pictures which the poet was concerned to produce in the minds of his readers. Some critics stress the desirability of the fully-formed image; others recognize the esthetic value of an economy of detail as leaving something for the imagination of the reader to complete. Still others realized that no precise rule could be drawn, and that both methods of procedure had been effective on occasion.

Joseph Warton heads the list of those critics who favor the fully-formed image. According to Warton,

THE use, the force, and the excellence of language, certainly consists in raising, *clear, complete,* and *circumstantial* images, and in turning *readers* into *spectators*.[23]

In *Windsor Forest,* Pope uses the classical device of the descent to Hades in connection with the blessings which the Peace of Utrecht will bring to England. Exiled by Peace to the infernal regions,

> In brazen bonds shall barb'rous Discord dwell;
> Gigantic Pride, pale Terror, gloomy Care,
> And mad Ambition, shall attend her there:
> There purple Vengeance bathed in gore retires,
> Her weapons blunted and extinct her fires:
> There hateful Envy her own snakes shall feel,
> And Persecution mourn her broken wheel:
> There Faction roar, Rebellion bite her chain,
> And gasping Furies thirst for blood in vain.[24]

Warton thought this "groupe of allegorical personages . . . worthy the pencil of Rubens or Julio Romano," but he wished "that the epithets barbarous (discord), mad (ambition), hateful (envy), had been particular and picturesque, instead of general and indiscriminating," although Virgil, too (whose figures at the gate to Hades in the sixth book of the *Aeneid* were in Pope's mind as he wrote), "has not always used such adjuncts and epithets as a painter or statuary might work after; he says only *ultrices* CURAE, *mortiferum* BELLUM. . . ." Hence Warton concludes that "in this famous passage, Virgil has exhibited no images so lively and distinct, as these living figures painted by POPE, each of them with their proper insignia and attributes."[25] Again, in Pope's imitation of Spenser, Warton complains that Pope's figures of

Obloquy, Slander, Envy and Malice, are not marked with any distinct attributes, they are not those living figures, whose attributes and behaviour Spenser has minutely drawn with so much clearness and truth, that we behold them with our eyes, as plainly as we do on the cieling [*sic*] of the banquetting-house.[26]

Clearly, Warton favors the fully-formed image: Lucretius, he notes with approval, is a "SCULPTOR-POET. His images have a bold relief."[27]

Like his brother Joseph, Thomas Warton was an admirer of the personifications of Spenser, and a great part of his admiration stems from his predilection for minutely detailed images. Spenser's delineations of "FEAR, ENVY, FANCY, DESPAIR, and the like" are superior to similar beings in Ariosto because Spenser "painted these figures so fully and distinctly."[28]

Richard Hurd was another critic who stressed the importance of the fully-formed image. True poetical genius

is what we call *painting* in poetry; by which not only the general natures of things are described, and their appearances shadowed forth; but every single *property* marked, and the poet's own image set in distinct *relief* before the view of his reader.[29]

The objects which poetry describes may be conceived by all poets. It is the manner of writing them down that distinguishes the genius from the second-rate poet. It is genius when,

as Longinus well expresses it . . . "the poet, from his own vivid and enthusiastic conception seems to have the object, he describes, in actual view, and presents it, almost, to the eyes of the reader."[30]

A number of critics, however, stress the value of the image in which only one or two details are mentioned as leaving something for the imagination of the reader to complete. Both poets and painters, according to Hildebrand Jacob,

never gratify more the Observers of their *Works,* than when they express themselves not so fully, but that these may find Matter enough to exercise their own *Imaginations* upon: We are agreeably flatter'd by such *Discoveries*.[31]

Daniel Webb compared the images of Shakespeare

to those drawings of the capital Painters, in which, though the parts are often rather *hinted* than made out, yet the ideas are compleat; they both give a delightful exercise to our minds, in continuing and enlarging the design.[32]

James Beattie recognized the value of both positions. He agreed with the "acknowledged truth in criticism" that "poetical description ought to be distinct and lively, and such as might both assist the fancy, and direct the hand, of the painter." He agreed too that "the best poets are the most picturesque." But he asks if all poetry should be picturesque, and finds that it should not, for to the right imitation of nature, shade is necessary, as well as light. We may be powerfully affected by that which is not visible at all; and of visible things some cannot be, and many ought not to be, painted: and the mind is often better pleased with images of its own forming, or finishing, than with those that are set before it complete in all their colours and proportions.[33]

It is significant that the emphasis on the importance of distinct and picturesque imagery is especially pronounced in the writings of the Warton brothers and Richard Hurd, three critics who favor poetry in which the imagination is much "indulged." Joseph Warton's preface to his *Odes on Several Subjects* (1746) may be regarded as the manifesto of a group of mid-century poets and critics who emphasize the importance of imagination in poetry. "The public," writes Warton,

has been so much accustomed of late to didactic poetry alone, and essays on moral subjects, that any work where the imagination is much indulged will perhaps not be relished or regarded. The author therefore of these pieces is in some pain lest certain austere critics should think them too fanciful and descriptive. But as he is convinced that the fashion of moralizing in verse has been carried too far, and as he looks upon invention and imagination to be the chief faculties of a poet, so he will be happy if the following odes may be looked upon as an attempt to bring back poetry into its right channel.[34]

In Warton we behold the theorist of the movement, in William Collins the poet who carried practice to a level of excellence not reached by other mid-century writers of "fanciful" poetry. Personification is a prominent feature in the verse of Joseph Warton, and the odes of Collins are notable for their vividly pictorialized abstractions. The frequent use of the figure in the verse of the Warton brothers was a cause of regret to Thomas Quayle. In common with most critics of the late nineteenth and early twentieth centuries, Quayle saw in the Wartons "two men who, crudely, perhaps, but nevertheless unmistakably, adumbrated the Romantic doctrine." Quayle found "a certain irony" in the fact that the Wartons "should have been among the foremost to indulge in an

excess against which later the avowed champion of Romanticism
[Wordsworth] was to inveigh with all his power."[35] The fact is
that the frequent use of personified abstractions in the poetry of
the Wartons and Collins is a direct outcome of their enthusiasm
for a poetry of "imagination" as opposed to poetry which was
considered to appeal less to the poetic fancy than to the "prosaic"
understanding. Imagination-fancy commonly refers, in the eighteenth century, to the act of mind which produced the sylphs and
gnomes in Pope's *Rape of the Lock* rather than to the type of imaginative organization so brilliantly displayed in the *Epistle to
Arbuthnot*. The personified abstraction was equally the product
of that creative faculty of mind which invents beings "out of
nature." In language reminiscent of Addison's, Joseph Warton
refers to Caliban as the creation of Shakespeare's "own imagination, in the formation of which he could derive no assistance from
observation or experience."[36] Pope's sylphs are said to be "conceived and carried on . . . with vast exuberance of fancy."[37]
But the prosopopoeia also, if "conducted with dignity and propriety, may be justly esteemed one of the greatest efforts of the
creative power of a warm and lively imagination."[38] Few poets
could aspire to the creation of an Ariel, a sylph, or a Caliban;[39]
many, however, could indulge their imaginations in the fabrication of beautiful or significant personifications. It is not surprising, therefore, that the personified abstraction should figure
prominently in "fanciful" poetry or that mid-century poets and
critics should be inclined to stress the creative element involved
in the act of personifying. Like Shakespeare's Caliban, the personified abstraction was a "fiction"; the product, therefore, of
"original" invention.

Imagery, said Robert Andrews, a mid-century writer of odes
addressed to abstractions, constitutes the essence of poetry, "so
that the more or less any composition has of it, it has the more or
less of Poetry."[40] He uses the words "creative description" in referring to

objects that never at all exist but in the poet's imagination, as HOM-ER's Gods and Goddesses, the Muses, Fairies, Genii of places, the Virtues and Vices personified, and all the other branches of the poetical machinery.[41]

John Ogilvie, another writer of odes to abstractions, regards them as the product of the "creative imagination,"[42] and thinks them peculiarly appropriate to lyric poetry as that form in which the fancy reigned supreme. In the ode, said Ogilvie, "we are highly entertained with frequent personifications, as these are the criterions by which we estimate the genius of the Poet."[43] Another critic uses the word "invention" in referring to the process of mind responsible for the fabrication of personified abstractions. Allegory, he says,

gives great latitude to genius, and affords such a boundless scope for invention, that the poet is allowed to soar beyond all creation; to give life and action to virtues, vices, passions, diseases, and natural and moral qualities.[44]

The ode, according to Joseph Warton, should be characterized by "imagery, figures, and poetry" rather than by "delicate sentiment, and philosophical reflection."[45] The essence of poetry is equated with imagery and figures, that is, with descriptive effects rather than with the didactic content inherent in the neoclassic poetry of "statement." Warton thought the personified abstraction a "great beauty" in lyric poetry,[46] largely because he regarded it as the product of the creative imagination and therefore appropriate to a species of poetry in which the fancy predominated. Spenser had personified Pain, Strife, Revenge, and other abstract entities in the second and third books of the *Faerie Queene*. "Here," said Warton, "all is in life and motion; here we behold the true Poet or MAKER; this is creation."[47]

I have mentioned Andrews and Ogilvie as writers of odes addressed to abstractions. The ode was associated throughout the eighteenth century with imaginative "enthusiasm." But as it existed in the earlier years of the century, the ode was not a form

conducive to the type of imaginative expression favored by the
Wartons and by those who held similar views concerning the importance of imagination-fancy in poetry. At the end of the seventeenth century most writers identified the ode with the Cowleyan
pindaric, and the form was popular among lesser poets of the
early eighteenth century, attaining perhaps its greatest vogue during the decade 1710-20.[48] These odes represented contemporary
efforts to capture the "enthusiasm" and "nobility" of Pindar. As
such, they were supposed to exhibit "Nobleness of Thought, Elevation, and Transport."[49] The subject matter was varied. Many
pindarics were written on religious themes, others were written
to celebrate the virtues of kings and great men, or to commemo-
rate some event in the current history of the nation. When the
influence of Longinus began to make itself felt in England, the
pindaric immediately acquired a reputation for sublimity, since
the qualities formerly attributed to it were precisely those Longinus had associated with the sublime. The quality of sublimity is
associated with the ode throughout the century, especially if it
assumes pindaric form, but the objects which formerly seemed
best fitted to stimulate the sublime imagination of the poet are
not those which mid-century odists favored as conducive to what
an admirer of Collins called "a wild sublimity of fancy."[50] The
basic difference between the earlier pindaric and the mid-century
ode is well brought out by Richard Shepherd in the preface to his
Odes Descriptive and Allegorical. "Of the descriptive and allegorical Ode," says Shepherd,

the Writings of the Ancients afford no Examples. . . . This Spe-
cies of Writing is in almost every Circumstance different from the
Pindarick Ode, which has its Foundation in Fact and Reality, that
Fact worked up and heightened by a studied Pomp and Grandeur of
Expression; it not only admits of, but requires bold Digressions,
abrupt and hasty Transitions: while the other is built intirely upon
Fancy, and Ease and Simplicity of Diction are its peculiar Char-
acteristicks.[51]

The descriptive and allegorical ode "is built intirely upon Fancy,"

that is, upon "fiction" as opposed to "Fact and Reality." It is "de-
signed ultimately to display not so much the power of the subject
addressed as the power of the poet's imagination."[52] The earlier
pindaric or "Great Ode" had been "a fragmentary plot, involving
a leading character and a single act or selection of acts to reveal
his attributes," whereas the later allegorical ode is "a creation of
the 'imagination,' substituting the poet's personifications for external persons and events."[53]

The Cowleyan pindaric had been discredited by the ineptness
of many of its practitioners, to say nothing of the inherent weaknesses of the form itself, nor did its spirit or subject matter appeal
to those who wished to write poems "built intirely upon Fancy."
It is significant that the rise in popularity of "odes descriptive and
allegorical" coincides with the growth of interest in Milton's
L'Allegro and *Il Penseroso.* The distinction which Addison had
elaborated between prose as a product of the understanding and
poetry as a product of the imagination assumes a new significance
with the rise in influence and reputation of Spenser, and especially of Milton. E. R. Wasserman regards Spenser "as the poet
who, perhaps more than any other, had exhibited that fancy and
image-making faculty which the neoclassicists almost universally
granted to be the essence of poetry."[54] The same could be said of
the Milton of *L'Allegro* and *Il Penseroso.* One critic admired
Milton's octosyllabics

for the frequent and beautiful use the poet has made of the figure
called *Prosopopoeia;* by which he has personified almost every object
in his view, raised a great number of pleasing images, and introduced
qualities and things inanimate as living and rational beings.[55]

The imagery in *Il Penseroso* is "not only poetry, but painting and
statuary; and you see, as it were in substance, the things which he
describes." The figure of Melancholy, for instance, in *Il Penseroso,* is "a perfect picture."[56] Another mid-century critic emphasizes the creative power which Milton showed in his personifica-

tions. Milton, in his description of "loathed Melancholy" in *L'Allegro,*

makes darkness *visible,* by the bold creation of another personage, whose whole power in possessing the imagination with false fears and ideal dangers, he fully expresses by one happy epithet.

Where brooding darkness spreads her JEALOUS wings.

The poet who thus gives a *local habitation* to Melancholy, in the like adventurous manner assigns to Mirth, parents, being, form, corporeal and mental qualities.[57]

It was this element of pictorial "creation" which made Milton's octosyllabics attractive to the Wartons and to other poets who were searching for a mode of lyric utterance which would give more scope to the play of imagination-fancy than the pindaric as usually written. James Thomson, Thomas Parnell, and Nicholas Rowe, among others, had written poems which show the influence of *L'Allegro* and *Il Penseroso,*[58] but the vogue for odes addressed to personified abstractions "appears to have begun about 1742 with the elder Warton, Gray, and Collins." "The spark," says R. D. Havens,

almost certainly came from *Allegro* and *Penseroso,* for the odes to personified qualities were under a very heavy debt to the structure, phraseology, and content of Milton's octosyllabics.[59]

The debt to Milton is sufficiently obvious in these stanzas from the elder Warton's poem entitled *Retirement: An Ode:*

> Joy, rose-lipp'd dryad, loves to dwell
> In sunny field or mossy cell,
> Delights on echoing hills to hear
> The reaper's song or lowing steer;
> Or view with tenfold plenty spread
> The crowded cornfield, blooming mead;
> While beauty, health, and innocence
> Transport the eye, the soul, the sense.
>
> . . . .
>
> Nymphs of the grove, in green array'd,
> Conduct me to your thickest shade,

> Deep in the bosom of the vale,
> Where haunts the lonesome nightingale;
> Where Contemplation, maid divine,
> Leans against some aged pine,
> Wrapp'd in steadfast thought profound,
> Her eyes fix'd steadfast on the ground.[60]

Sometimes the Miltonic structure is closely imitated, as in Richard Shepherd's ode *To Health,* in which we have the banishment of Disease:

> Hence meagre pale Disease,
> From the crude Banquets of Intemperance bred—

followed by the invocation to Hygeia:

> And come, *Hygeia,* bland and fair—

The enjoyments and various pursuits of Hygeia are then described.[61] But the significance of Milton, for the purposes of this book, does not lie in the fact that *L'Allegro* and *Il Penseroso* inspired a great number of imitations, but in the fact that these poems were a potent factor in stimulating a more extensive use of picturesquely detailed abstractions in the ode and in other poems in which the imagination was "much indulged." "In Warton," as A. S. P. Woodhouse says, "and more especially in Collins, the allegorical *is* the descriptive." The personifications of these poets are introduced "as occasions for pictorial descriptions."[62] The higher levels of imaginative exertion are closely identified with "picturesque" descriptive effects. Joseph Warton's *Ode to Fancy* provides an example of personification in the Miltonic manner. As one might expect from our review of Warton's critical opinions, the goddess Fancy is vividly pictorialized:

> O nymph with loosely-flowing hair,
> With buskin'd leg, and bosom bare,
> Thy waist with myrtle-girdle bound,
> Thy brows with Indian feathers crown'd,
> Waving in thy snowy hand
> An all-commanding magic wand,

> Of pow'r to bid fresh gardens blow,
> 'Mid cheerless Lapland's barren snow,
> Whose rapid wings thy flight convey
> Through air, and over earth and sea,
> While the vast, various landscape lies
> Conspicuous to thy piercing eyes.
> O lover of the desart, hail![63]

Havens detects the influence of Milton's octosyllabics on this poem,[64] but in regard to the figure of Fancy herself, the Miltonic influence is pervasive rather than specific, revealing itself in Warton's picturesque manner of presentation.

Sometimes a whole train of allegorical figures is introduced, each figure with its "proper insignia and attributes." The enthusiast in Warton's poem of that name justifies his love of primitive nature by associating urban sophistication with immorality and suffering. He personifies the virtues that are to accompany his retirement to primitive America where "beneath a plantain's shade/. . . Happiness and Quiet sit enthron'd." It is a moonlit night, and the enthusiast wanders "musing" along some "level mead," invoking "Contemplation sage" to lift his soul "above this little earth" that he may hear the "tuneful turning spheres," or see, as in a vision, "the little Fays that dance in neighbouring dales." When the enthusiast's faculties have been attuned to this state of trancelike receptiveness, the vision duly appears:

> . . . lo, what awful forms
> Yonder appear! sharp-ey'd Philosophy
> Clad in dun robes, an eagle on his wrist,
> First meets my eye; next, virgin Solitude
> Serene, who blushes at each gazer's sight;
> Then Wisdom's hoary head, with crutch in hand,
> Trembling, and bent with age; last, Virtue's self,
> Smiling, in white array'd, who with her leads
> Sweet Innocence, that prattles by her side,
> A naked boy!—Harass'd with fear, I stop,
> I gaze, when Virtue thus—"Whoe'er thou art,
> Mortal, by whom I deign to be beheld
> In these my midnight-walks; depart, and say

> That henceforth I and my immortal train
> Forsake Britannia's isle; who fondly stoops
> To Vice, her favourite Paramour."—She spoke,
> And as she turn'd, her round and rosy neck,
> Her flowing train, and long ambrosial hair,
> Breathing rich odours, I enamour'd view.[65]

It is evident that Warton's attitude toward the personified abstraction closely parallels that of Addison. The enthusiast is, by contemporary definition, a man of vehement feelings, prone to "flights" of imagination. The allegorical figures appear to him when he is in a state of visionary exaltation. Such vision comes only to one whose soul has been lifted, momentarily at least, "above this little earth." The vision itself is vividly pictorialized. It is intended to appeal to the "picture-receiving, picture-retaining" faculty of mind.

What is said here of Warton's allegorical figures is true also of the vividly pictorialized abstractions which appear in the odes of William Collins. The odes of Collins, taken as a whole, represent the most thoroughgoing attempt in eighteenth-century poetry at the evocation of images "without any foundation in reality."[66] This was the result of Collins's wholehearted acceptance of the Wartonian pronouncement that "invention and imagination" are the "chief faculties of a poet." The difference between Collins and Joseph Warton lies in the passionate intensity with which the former reacted to beliefs held in common by both men. The result is that the odes of Collins may stand as the most perfect exemplification in eighteenth-century poetry of what Addison called the fairy way of writing.

Like his contemporaries, Collins emphasizes the picture-making function of imagination-fancy. In the *Ode on the Poetical Character,* the magic girdle, representing the true poetic power, is granted to few. "Young Fancy,"

> To few the God-like Gift assigns,
> To gird their blest prophetic Loins,
> And gaze her Visions wild, and feel unmix'd her Flame![67]

To Collins true poetry was a product of "Young Fancy," or the imagination, and the chief function of the poetic imagination lay in its power of evoking "visions wild."

But Collins was too great a lover of the praeternatural to rest content with a terrestrial origin for "visions wild." He wished to exalt the praeternatural element that he so admired in the poetry of Shakespeare, Spenser, and Milton. In his *Ode on the Poetical Character* the wish becomes father to the thought. In this ode true poetry is represented as the child of Heaven and Fancy. There is a quality of visionary intensity in Collins's poetry which leads one to believe that this statement of a divine origin is something more than conventional homage paid to the Muse of Poetry. A. S. P. Woodhouse sees Collins as a rebel against the world of "actual experience":

Collins, it would seem, conceives his "persons" as creatures of the spirit-world. They are revealed to him in a sort of vision. With them move other visitants from the same regions, the demons who preside over nature's cataclysms and mankind's crimes.[68]

Collins wishes to believe that there exists a spirit-world, and that it is the duty and privilege of the poet to make contact with this world, reproducing its phenomena in forms suitable to the comprehension of terrestrial beings. The praeternatural element in the poetry of Shakespeare, Spenser, and Milton seemed evidence that such contact had been made in the past, while the lack of this element in succeeding poetry appeared to show the difficulty of the task. If Addison, in contradiction to his theoretical principles, felt that factors of "Tradition, History and Observation" were unable wholly to account for praeternatural creations such as Shakespeare's Caliban, it is not surprising that Collins should reject the empirical explanation *in toto*. He does so, however, not by redefining the terms "imagination" and "fancy," as Coleridge was to do, but by making what is, after all, a logical deduction from conventional premises concerning the meaning of these terms. If fabrications such as Caliban could not be explained on the basis of the poet's experience of the actual world, then there must exist another source for the materials employed in the operations of imagination. The contemporary association of imagination-fancy with "fiction," plus Collins's own proneness to what Johnson called "flights of imagination" surpassing "the bounds of nature,"[69] suggested the obvious alternative. The "visions wild" of the poet must owe their conception to an inspiration from above. True poetry, therefore, is represented as the child of Heaven and Fancy:

The Band [i.e., the "magic girdle" representing true poetry] . . .
Was wove on that creating Day
When He, who call'd with Thought to Birth
Yon tented Sky, this laughing Earth,
And drest with Springs and Forests tall,
And pour'd the Main engirting all,
Long by the lov'd *Enthusiast* ["Fancy"] woo'd,
Himself in some Diviner Mood,
Retiring, sate with her alone,
And plac'd her on his Sapphire Throne,
The whiles, the vaulted Shrine around,
Seraphic Wires were heard to sound,
Now sublimest Triumph swelling,
Now on Love and Mercy dwelling;
And she, from out the veiling Cloud
Breath'd her magic Notes aloud:
And Thou, Thou rich-hair'd Youth of Morn [the Sun],
And all thy subject Life was born![70]

Mrs. Barbauld has a suggestive comment to make on this passage:

Probably the obscure idea that floated in the mind of the Author was this, that true Poetry, being a representation of Nature, must have its archetype in those ideas of the supreme mind which originally gave birth to Nature.[71]

If Mrs. Barbauld is right, Collins would think of his personifications as, in some sort, evocations in "sensible" form of those ideas of the supreme mind which "originally gave birth to Nature." These evocations would owe their ultimate existence to

the world of praeternatural reality in so far as they represented
the poet's visionary insight into the realm of archetypal "ideas."
Such vision could be attained only through the aid of divine inspiration and this had lately been withheld:

> . . . Heav'n, and *Fancy,* kindred Pow'rs,
> Have now o'erturn'd th'inspiring Bow'rs,
> Or curtain'd close such Scene from ev'ry future View.[72]

For purposes of exposition, I have discussed Collins's attitude
toward the imagination in terms of theory although it is highly
probable that this attitude remained with him a matter of feeling,
never thought out in strictly logical terms. The intensity of Collins's belief in the praeternatural as the element with which true
poetry deals leads him to endow this element with a reality of its
own, and to see the poet as intermediary between this world of
vision and the world of actual experience.

For the *"Fairy Way of Writing,"* said Addison, "a very odd
turn of Thought" is required, "and it is impossible for the Poet
to succeed in it, who has not a particular Cast of Fancy, and an
Imagination naturally fruitful and superstitious."[73] If one may
believe Johnson, Collins fulfilled these qualifications to an eminent degree. Collins, said Johnson,

had employed his mind chiefly upon works of fiction, and subjects of
fancy; and, by indulging some peculiar habits of thought, was eminently delighted with those flights of imagination which pass the
bounds of nature, and to which the mind is reconciled only by a passive acquiescence in popular traditions.[74]

The first strophe of the *Ode to Fear* provides an instance of Collins's aptitude for the fairy way of writing:

> THOU to whom the World unknown
> With all its shadowy Shapes is shown;
> Who see'st appall'd th'unreal Scene,
> While Fancy lifts the Veil between:
> > Ah *Fear!* ah frantic *Fear!*
> > I see, I see Thee near!

> I know thy hurried Step, thy haggard Eye!
> Like Thee I start, like Thee disorder'd fly,
> For lo what *Monsters* in thy Train appear!
> *Danger,* whose Limbs of Giant Mold
> What mortal Eye can fix'd behold?
> Who stalks his Round, an hideous Form,
> Howling amidst the Midnight Storm,
> Or throws him on the ridgy Steep
> Of some loose hanging Rock to sleep!
> And with him thousand Phantoms join'd,
> Who prompt to Deeds accurs'd the Mind:
> And those, the Fiends who near allied,
> O'er Nature's Wounds, and Wrecks preside;
> Whilst *Vengeance,* in the lurid Air,
> Lifts her red Arm, expos'd and bare:
> On whom that rav'ning Brood of Fate,
> Who lap the Blood of Sorrow, wait;
> Who, *Fear,* this ghastly Train can see,
> And look not madly wild, like Thee?[75]

Before the "shadowy shapes" of the "unreal" world may be seen by the poet, Fancy must lift the veil: the imagination must assume predominance over the rational faculty. The poet is then prepared for the dramatic appearance of Fear, Danger, and Vengeance. The abstractions are presented, not as "shadowy shapes," but as though they had a real existence of their own. The unreal scene is, in fact, vividly realized. Addison had associated the personified abstraction with "monsters" and other beings "out of nature"; in Collins's ode, Danger and Vengeance are monsters from another world as well as personifications of affective states common to human beings. To Addison, this "fairy" way of writing provided only one of the several pleasures of imagination which poetry affords, but to Collins it was the very essence of poetry itself. Whatever one may think of Collins's achievement, the intention is clear enough. The personified abstraction is to lose its "fictional" quality. The reader is invited to accept it as a real "person," a visitant from the spirit-world of the imagination.

In this chapter I have been concerned to show the importance of the personified abstraction in the verse of Joseph Warton, Collins, and other mid-century writers of poetry in which the imagination is "much indulged." I have tried to show why these poets think of the personified abstraction as a sign of imaginative "indulgence," and why it becomes, in their verse, something more than a means of conveying "particular circumstances" in an "unusual and entertaining Manner." In this poetry the personified abstraction is projected as a product of the higher levels of imaginative exertion. Whether or not the poet consciously attempts to achieve the heights of the imaginative sublime, he does at least lay claim to the projection of figures which are to be regarded as products of "vehement feelings." The emphasis on the figure in the verse of these poets stems from their identification of imagination-fancy with "fiction" as contrasted with objects, persons, or scenes of being which could be said to have a real existence in nature. But if it be granted that the personified abstraction is often of central importance in poems "built intirely upon Fancy," it is obvious that the figure occurs more frequently in eighteenth-century verse as a poetic ornament or "embellishment." It becomes a "short expression" which conveys an ordinary thought to the mind "in the most pleasing manner," and is to be regarded as aspiring to the condition of the "pleasant" or the "beautiful" rather than to the sublime, or even to the "fanciful," when this epithet refers to a prosopopoeia which is understood to be a product of "vehement feelings."

The modern reader is apt to find this incidental use of the figure especially irritating. Eighteenth-century critics may extol the value of "proper insignia and attributes," but the modern reader is apt to see only a deadening adherence to convention and a deplorable lack of originality. Time appears again and again as an old man with a scythe, Love as a beautiful boy with a bow and arrows, and Justice is never without the sword with which the ancients endowed her. In the next chapter I attempt to decide whether this lack of originality is due simply to a reverence for the forms these abstractions assumed in ancient art and literature, or whether there were not more cogent reasons for this adherence to convention in the matter of physical differentiae.

CHAPTER III

The Personified Abstraction as an "Object of Sight"

REVERENCE for the ancients was great throughout the century, and there was great respect for classical precedent in regard to the physical differentiae which distinguished each abstraction among the ancients. Studies of the remains of antiquity confirmed the relatively stable nature of these attributes. Thus Addison noted "that not only the Virtues, and the like imaginary persons, but all the heathen Divinities appear generally in the same Dress among the Poets that they wear in Medals."[1] Hope, Piety, Justice, and similar virtues are personified as females in eighteenth-century poetry because this was the practice of antiquity, due, as Addison says, to the fact that these substantives chanced to be of the feminine gender in the Latin language.[2] The practice of the ancients in regard to the insignia and attributes of their gods and goddesses appealed to the neoclassic preference for clarity and decorum in literary matters. In his paraphrase of Prodicus' apologue, *The Choice of Hercules,* Addison expresses his admiration for

the speeches of these ladies [Prodicus' figures of Virtue and Vice, or Pleasure], as containing in them the chief arguments for a life of virtue, or a life of pleasure, that could enter into the thoughts of an heathen,

but he is particularly pleased

with the different figures he [Prodicus] gives the two goddesses. Our modern authors have represented Pleasure or Vice with an alluring face, but ending in snakes and monsters. Here she appears in all the charms of beauty, though they are all false and borrowed: and by that means composes a vision entirely natural and pleasing.[3]

Admiration for the allegorical figures of the ancients extends beyond the sphere of academic interest to the realm of practical application. The *Tabula* of Cebes contains the account of a beautiful allegorical painting, and its author emphasizes the didactic value of this type of pictorial description. In Cebes critics found an exemplification of the intimate relationship which might exist between painting and literature. Inspired by the "picture" of Cebes, critics propose literary personifications as proper models for pictorial imitation. The dialoguists in Shaftesbury's treatise entitled *The Moralists* indulge in much speculation concerning the ways in which the different virtues might be drawn "after the ancient manner." They pursue this task "till Prodicus and Cebes, and all the ancients [are] exhausted."[4] Shaftesbury devotes some thirty pages to *A Notion of the Historical Draught or Tablature of the Judgment of Hercules, according to Prodicus*. This is a serious manual of instruction to the aspiring painter, replete with details concerning "perspective," "drapery," and the "ornaments of the piece."[5] Shaftesbury's disciple, John Gilbert Cooper, follows his master in describing imaginary pictures drawn from the "designs" of Cebes and Prodicus, strongly recommending them to the attention of those contemporary artists who wished to see "natural and moral Beauty . . . again united as they were of old."[6] The seriousness with which such proposals were urged may be seen from James Moor's vigorous denial that the painting described in the *Tabula* of Cebes was too crowded with figures for successful imitation on canvas. Moor insists that Cebes' picture could be reproduced without the slightest violation of the strictest laws of pictorial composition.[7]

Shaftesbury insists upon the "just *simplicity,* and *unity*" which the painter of Prodicus' apologue must achieve,[8] and it was perhaps inevitable that the practice of the ancients in this respect

should be compared with that of the "moderns" to the frequent
disadvantage of the latter. In the eighteenth century the *Faerie
Queene* was the chief example of "modern" allegorical practice.
The difference between classical and Spenserian practice in regard to allegorical description is very clearly brought out by
Joseph Spence in his *Polymetis*. Spenser's allegorical figures are
criticized because they "fall very short of that simplicity and propriety which is so remarkable in the works of the antients." Certain of Spenser's figures are "too complicated, or over-done";
there are too many "things" or attributes about them.[9] Economy
of presentation is a desirable quality in itself: Spence praises the
ancients because they were often successful in lending allegorical
significance to their figures through the attribution of a single,
well-chosen descriptive detail. This is in striking contrast to the
"multiplicity of marks" with which the moderns adorn their abstractions.[10] In Spenser the moral is too often obscured by the
poet's lavishness in regard to details of description. The figures
of Doubt, Hope, and Pleasure in book three of the *Faerie Queene*
"are not well marked out"; that is, the physical insignia do not
tend to illuminate the allegorical parallel.[11] Spence concludes that
if the English poet had formed his allegorical figures on the plan
of the ancient artists and poets, he would have followed nature
more closely, and been less often plunged into "inconsistent imaginations."[12] Spence, indeed, criticizes the ancients themselves,
and their imitators, for a lack of precision in their accounts of
allegorical deities. The personifications of Dawn based upon
Homer's account of Aurora and her chariot leave Spence with a
feeling of irritation. What is the color of Dawn's robe, he asks,
how many horses pull her chariot, and what are the colors of the
horses? Different poets have given different answers, but, says
Spence, "the greatest criticks have ever thought, that *consistency*
is requir'd in the most *unbounded fictions*."[13]

In eighteenth-century poetry, such consistency as there is in the
matter of allegorical "attributes and insignia" may be explained,
in part, as a natural result of the general tendency to make the

antique, or pseudo-antique, an integral part of the contemporary setting. We adorn our houses with the statues of Greece and Rome, said Joseph Warton, just as we enrich our compositions with their "sentiments and images."[14] The pagan deities

appeared frequently in the paintings of Reynolds and his contemporaries, they stood or reclined upon the outside of public buildings and filled niches in the interior, they wriggled their way into chairs and tables and beds, they warmed themselves on fire-places, they hunted or caroused on tapestries and urns and screens, and to the dismay of some Christians they even penetrated into the parish church in the more elaborate monuments erected to ladies and gentlemen deceased.

James Sutherland concludes that

if the pagan gods had not become fully naturalized in eighteenth-century England, they entered much more fully into the consciousness of the educated Englishman than they do to-day. He first met them as a schoolboy in Ovid and Virgil and in the copperplates of Tooke's *Pantheon,* and he was continually reminded of them in later life as a part of his cultural heritage.[15]

The eighteenth century paid quite as much attention to the allegorical as to the ornamental function of such deities. Robert Dodsley concludes his description of Shenstone's estate at "The Leasowes" with the account of a statue of the Medicean Venus "beside a bason of goldfish, encompassed round with shrubs," and illustrated with a poetic inscription which draws a parallel between the appearance of the statue and the sort of landscape exemplified at "The Leasowes." It is not the martial or the amorous Venus which Shenstone celebrates, but the Venus who rises "'from the foamy tide,"

> While half withdrawn she seems to hide,
> And half reveals, her charms.

The statue neatly (if somewhat indecorously) symbolizes the effect of "sweet concealment" which Shenstone sought to achieve at his *ferme ornée:*

> Let sweet concealment's magic art
> Your mazy bounds invest;
> And while the sight unveils a part,
> Let fancy paint the rest.[16]

Pope writes that his grotto at Twickenham wants "nothing to complete it but a good statue with an inscription." Such a statue would serve as a symbol of the grotto as a whole; it would act to personify "the aquatic idea of the whole place."[17] Joseph Warton compares the kind of pleasure which such landscape statuary imparts to the pleasure one receives from the insertion by the poet of "oblique" moral reflections in passages of scenic description. The poet Dyer, viewing the countryside from the top of Grongar Hill, reflects on the seeming minuteness of the landscape below:

> How close and small the Hedges lie,
> What Streaks of Meadows cross the Eye!

and goes on to point the moral—

> So, we mistake the future's face,
> Ey'd through hope's deluding glass;
> As yon summits soft and fair
> Clad in colours of the air,
> Which to those who journey near,
> Barren, brown, and rough appear.[18]

"THE unexpected insertion of such reflections," says Warton, "imparts to us the same pleasure that we feel, when in wandering through a wilderness or grove, we suddenly behold in the turning of the walk, a statue of some VIRTUE or MUSE."[19] Such statues pointed a moral in so far as they expressed in symbolic form the feelings or attitudes which a particular locality seemed to convey. The fondness for symbolic expression is carried to a further extreme when the man of taste disregards the natural character of the landscape in favor of a superimposed allegorical panorama, as Aaron Hill does in the outline of a projected rock-work for his garden. Hill plans to build four grottoes dedicated to Power,

Riches, Honour, and Learning. In the grotto dedicated to Power, there are to be

grotesque openings, each of which gives prospect to a different walk, through the wood, terminated by a figure, proper to the position: These are FAME, REVENGE, VICTORY, VIOLENCE, PRIDE, and SECURITY; the six most natural persuits [*sic*], in the attainments of POWER.[20]

I have discussed the poetry-painting parallel in the preceding chapter, and it has been seen how, in practice, the eighteenth-century reader tended to think of allegorical figures in poetry as "pictures" which were presumed to have the same effect on the mind as similar figures in painting. One result of the tendency to look for "the obvious characteristics of visual art" in poetry is the supposition that the poet must have modeled his image upon a statue, a painting, or some other material representation. Addison, noting that "not only the Virtues, and the like imaginary persons, but all the heathen Divinities appear generally in the same Dress among the Poets that they wear in Medals," thought that "both the one and the other took the Mode from the ancient *Greek* Statuaries."[21] Charles Lamotte thought the ancient poets remiss in not confessing their obligation to the painters and sculptors of antiquity. Virgil, he maintains, had made use in his descriptions of the "Antiques and Monuments" extant in his time.[22] William Gilpin thought that

it is much more probable, that the poet copied *forms* from the sculptor, who must be supposed to understand them better, from having studied them more; than that the sculptor should copy from the poet.[23]

Thomas Warton believed that Spenser's acquaintance with public "shews and spectacles" helped to make him an allegorical poet,[24] and, according to John Pinkerton, "modern" [i.e., Renaissance and medieval] personification originated from contemporary "Mysteries and Masques," while ancient personification seems to have sprung from the Religious Processions; and, in Rome especially, from the Triumphs, at which conquered Provinces, and the like, were represented with the most beautiful imagery of symbol.[25]

This constant reiteration of the parallel between poetic imagery and the visual arts, in all its many ramifications, has led some critics to suppose that the eighteenth-century reader was endowed with powers of visualization superior to those possessed by readers of the present day. E. R. Wasserman terms the modern visual imagination "sluggish" as compared with the eighteenth-century imagination, which "took fire," he says, with "far less" of "vivid objective details" than our own.[26] Cicely Davies believes that Joseph Warton's fondness for painting may have increased his powers of visualization.[27] Donald Davie comments on the "ready allegorical imagination" of the eighteenth-century reader, which, he says, "seems lost to us to-day."[28] Johnson, in the *Vanity of Human Wishes,* speaks of "the gen'ral Massacre of Gold":

> Wide-wasting Pest! that rages unconfin'd,
> And crowds with Crimes the Records of Mankind;
> For Gold his Sword the Hireling Ruffian draws,
> For Gold the hireling Judge distorts the Laws.[29]

Macdonald Emslie believes that these four lines are based upon the "familiar personification" of Justice:

The last pair shows that the figure of Justice with her drawn sword is behind what these four lines "state." The judge is equated with the ruffian, for both are hirelings, but *distorts* points to the absence in the judge of Justice's other functions, represented by her blindfold and her balance; then, in addition to the judge, Justice herself is in some degree made parallel with the ruffian, for both have only their drawn swords.[30]

One may not agree completely with Emslie's further detailed analysis of this passage, but his remarks as quoted do not seem wide of the mark, provided one grants the existence of a "ready" allegorical imagination among eighteenth-century readers.

One may agree with Davie concerning the existence of this allegorical imagination without going on to assume a fundamental difference between the eighteenth century and our own day so far as the ability to visualize is concerned. If many of the simple pictorial images in eighteenth-century verse make little impression upon us today, this is due, probably, to the fact that the verse itself fails to satisfy many of the expectations which we bring to poetry. If the poetry itself is not stimulating, the images which it contains will make little impression upon the reader, visually or otherwise. If we do not "see" these images as eighteenth-century readers saw them, this is due less, perhaps, to a loss of visualizing power than to the fact that we do not find these images significant in a larger sense. If contemporary readers had a more positive sense of their poetic value, one may account for this by the presence in eighteenth-century life and thought of factors which favored the development of certain expectations in regard to poetry which are no longer prevalent today.

Donald Davie maintains that "a symptom and, it may be, a cause" of the eighteenth-century allegorical sense "was the popularity of the allegorical history painting."[31] I submit that not only paintings, but statues, medals, and other material representations contributed to form in the contemporary reader a "ready allegorical imagination." Objects of this sort acted as both cause and symptom. The allegorical tendency in literature and in the arts is a symptom of the empirical attitude on the one hand, and a cause of the development of a ready allegorical imagination on the other. As symptom, the allegorical mood is a result of the contemporary distrust of the vague and the indefinite, a distrust which carries with it a tendency to materialize the abstract wherever possible. On the other hand, the eighteenth-century reader's acquaintance with the allegorical mode in the representative arts would have the effect of stimulating his powers of visualization. Personifications in poetry would suggest their pro-

totypes in art. The bare mention of one or two details of dress or
insignia would be sufficient to stimulate a more or less complete
mental "picture," since the reader could be trusted to have a general idea of the appearance of the figure as a whole through his
acquaintance with contemporary art. In this way the physical differentiae associated with each abstraction would become, "not
empty clichés," but "the necessary and expected symbols to evoke
the proper image-making response."[32] Such an assumption helps
to explain the adherence to tradition in the matter of physical insignia. The eighteenth-century poet could count upon the use of
well-known detail to stimulate the formation of more or less distinct mental pictures. Any great divergence from tradition in the
case of the better-known allegorical figures would cause confu-
sion of imagery, defeating the purposes of the poet as well as the
expectations of the reader. To describe Justice personified, for
instance, with a spear instead of a sword, would be to reject a traditional image, dignified by the sanction of time, in favor of a
new one which could not be expected to convey the emotional
overtones associated with the image of convention. For these reasons the eighteenth-century reader would be inclined to agree
with William Melmoth that

to represent natural, moral, or intellectual qualities and affections as
persons, and appropriate to them those general emblems by which
their powers and properties are usually typified in pagan theology,
may be allowed as one of the most pleasing and graceful figures of
poetical rhetoric.[33]

Certain of the more familiar abstractions appear to have been
thought of as having a sort of independent existence of their own.
One should remember, in this connection, that eighteenth-century empiricism strongly implied the materialization of the abstract as a necessary act involved in any perception of "intellectual
objects." "To beings of more exalted faculties," said Thomas
Reid, "intellectual objects may, perhaps, appear to most advantage in their naked simplicity. But we can hardly conceive them

but by means of some analogy they bear to objects of sense."[34] The physical differentiae associated with each abstraction in sculpture, painting, and in the minor representative arts, as well as in literature, had the effect of lending an air of concrete solidity to the abstraction in question. There are some allegorical figures, said Erasmus Darwin,

which we have so often heard described or seen delineated, that we almost forget that they do not exist in common life; and thence view them without astonishment; as the figures of the heathen mythology, of angels, devils, death, and time; and almost believe them to be realities, even when they are mixed with representations of the natural forms of man.[35]

Uvedale Price speaks of Envy and Revenge as acknowledged "by all" to be "distinct characters":

Nay both of them, as well as many of our better affections, have been so often personified by poets, and imbodied by painters and sculptors, that we have as little doubt of their distinct figurative existence, as of the real existence of any of our acquaintance, and almost know them as readily.[36]

The eighteenth-century reader appears to have acquired the habit of associating each abstraction with certain "characteristic" insignia, regardless of whether or not such insignia appeared in the representations of antiquity. According to John Ogilvie,

We are . . . naturally taught to distinguish properly the insignia of imaginary creatures. Thus Fear is always known by her bristled Hair, Admiration by his erected Eyes, Time has his Scythe and his Hour-glass, and Fortune (unchangeable in one sense) stands blind on the Globe, to which she was exalted by Cebes.[37]

Ogilvie does not derive this tendency from the practice of imitating the ancients, in spite of his mention of Cebes: "we are," he says, *"naturally* taught to distinguish properly the insignia of imaginary creatures."

It has been seen that the practice of the ancients in this respect seemed "natural" chiefly because the physical differentiae associated with their deities happened to satisfy contemporary demands for perfect clarity and intelligibility in literary matters. In other words, the insignia in question were obvious in an allegorical sense. In instances in which the ancients, or tradition generally, had laid down certain easily comprehensible "marks" distinguishing this or that figure, the eighteenth-century poet was usually careful to follow in the footsteps of his predecessors in order to take advantage of the emotional overtones and image-making powers which such differentiae possessed. But where tradition was silent in the matter of "characteristic" insignia, the eighteenth-century poet felt free to invent his own, provided he chose only those obvious "marks" which his readers could be trusted to accept as the "natural" insignia of the figure in question. There is a revealing passage in Archibald Alison's *Essay on Taste* in regard to this question of physical differentiae. "We love," says Alison,

the dazzling White of Complexion of the infant in its cradle. We love afterwards the firm brown of Colour which distinguishes the young adventurer in exercise or arms. In the recluse student, we expect the pale Complexion, which signifies watching, and midnight meditation. In the soldier and sailor we look for a Complexion hardened to climate, and embrowned with honourable toil. In all the variety of classes into which society has distributed mankind, we look for, in the same manner, some distinct Colouring as significant of this classification. We meet with it in the descriptions of the Poet, and the representations of the Painter, and we feel our minds unsatisfied if we do not discover it in real life.[38]

If expectations of this sort were at all prevalent in regard to men and women in real life, it is easy to believe that comparable expectations would prevail even more strongly in regard to the allegorical "fictions" of the poet. The latter were avowedly symbolic; the eighteenth-century reader would expect them to bear the evident "marks" of their symbolic function.

Much of the irritation of the modern reader at the allegorical set-pieces of the eighteenth-century poets stems from their obviousness. Images, it is often felt today, should be striking; they should jolt the reader into attention. Modern readers, it has been said, must have "quickening particulars" at any cost.[39] The reader of today finds little that is vivid or stimulating in the attribution of such obvious characteristics as "rosy cheeks" to a figure of Health, or of "down-cast eyes" to an image of Modesty. The epithets appear superfluous because we are less prone to attach poetic value to purely pictorial qualities. To the eighteenth-century reader, however, such epithets served as aids to visualization. We wish the descriptive epithet to indicate more directly the sort of effect which the image is to convey; the eighteenth-century reader was content to let the effect of the image appear through the character of the mental picture which he expected it to stimulate. The power of forming such pictures was developed in some readers to a point where quite distinct visual images were evidently experienced from passages which contain a relatively slight element of particularized description. James Thomson personifies the "Power of Cultivation" as follows:

> O vale of bliss! O softly swelling hills!
> On which the Power of Cultivation lies,
> And joys to see the wonders of his toil.[40]

"We cannot conceive," says a writer in the *British Magazine,*

a more beautiful image than that of the Genius of Agriculture distinguished by the implements of his art, embrowned with labor, glowing with health, crowned with a garland of foliage, flowers and fruit, lying stretched at ease on the brow of a gentle swelling hill, and contemplating with pleasure the happy effects of his own industry.[41]

The critic, as Donald Davie says, "contributes much that is unsaid by Thomson," including, it may be noted, the "implements" or insignia proper to the Genius of Agriculture. It is true, however, that the critic "probably contributes nothing that was not in Thomson's intention."[42] Thomson wished his readers to visualize his abstraction in this fashion, and he knew he would not have to spell out his figure in full before such visualization could occur. A few hints upon which the imagination could build were all that was necessary. Such an instance supports the contention that the eighteenth-century allegorical imagination "took fire" with far less of vivid detail than our own.

There can be no doubt that for some people now, as in the eighteenth century, the picture-making function of poetry is by far the most important factor in their appreciation of this form of literature. Psychologists have investigated "imaginal reactions" to literature, and some have distinguished a so-called "plastic" type of imagination as against what has been called a "diffluent or emotional imagination." Persons possessing the first type of imagination are inclined to translate what they read into sharply defined visual images; the "diffluent" imagination, on the other hand, "would make things the symbols of vague infinities." The plastic imagination would perceive a poetic description of the rainbow as "a band of seven translucent colours to be delicately sensed and copied [in imagination]"; the diffluent would perceive the same object as "a mystery, a bridge from one Unknown World to another."[43]

The plastic imagination enjoys clear and distinct images; it rebels, therefore, at the incomplete prosopopoeia. Pope had written:

> Love, Hope, and Joy, fair pleasure's smiling train,
> Hate, Fear, and Grief, the family of pain;
> These mix'd with art, and to due bounds confin'd,
> Make and maintain the balance of the mind.[44]

Joseph Warton comments:

THIS beautiful group of allegorical personages, so strongly contrasted, how do they act? The prosopopeia is unfortunately dropped, and the metaphor changed immediately in the succeeding lines.[45]

There seems scarcely enough vivid detail in these lines to stimulate the picture-making faculty of the modern reader to any significant degree. It is evident, however, that Warton perceived these entities as persons rather than as qualities, and that the dropping of the prosopopoeia in line three had the effect of dissolving the mental picture already formed, or in process of formation.

Thomas Quayle found that the most prevalent type of eighteenth-century personfication is represented by the "mere abstraction," sometimes "qualified by epithets suggestive of human attributes, but [in which] there is little or no attempt to give a definite picture or evoke a distinctive image." Abstractions of this sort "swarm especially . . . in the odes of the mid-century."[46] The majority of Thomas Gray's personifications are of this type: "Nothing is visualized: we see no real image before us."[47]

But, as I have shown, eighteenth-century readers appear to have had little difficulty in "seeing" many of these abstractions. Of the major factors responsible for this state of affairs, there is, first, the tendency, fostered by contemporary empiricism, to objectify the abstract wherever possible; secondly, the emphasis on the parallel between the representative arts and the art of poetry; and, finally, the naturalization of the antique or pseudo-antique as an integral part of the eighteenth-century setting.

The effect of all this extends beyond any consideration of this or that figure of speech. It is seen in the prevailing eighteenth-century notion of what poetry sets out to do. "THE common notion of the power of poetry and eloquence, as well as that of words in ordinary conversation," says Edmund Burke, "is, that they affect the mind by raising in it ideas [images] of those things for which custom has appointed them to stand."[48] Burke finds, however, on a "diligent examination" of his own mind and "getting others to consider theirs," that the contrary is most often true; that the common effect of poetry is not to raise "ideas" of things.[49] This may be going too far, for as a recent critic has said,

we cannot . . . be sure that words perform their work in entire independence of the images of sense whose place they have so largely come to take; and it is not, I think, rash to think that they do not. No doubt clear imagery falls away to be replaced by words;

but it is exceedingly difficult to be sure that imagery of this kind
falls entirely away. Even when, for example, we are reading quickly,
it is presumptuous to conclude that no imagery, dim as we will, of
things is not present. Introspection cannot catch the mind as we
should like, and we need to be careful not to be too sure.[50]

We should agree with Burke, however, that many of the most
valuable effects of poetry derive from a use of language which
is immediately emotive rather than immediately picturesque.
Abstract words in particular gather around them certain associa-
tions, so that

being applied in . . . a variety of cases . . . we know readily by
habit to what things they belong, [and] they produce in the mind,
whenever they are afterwards mentioned, effects similar to those of
their occasions. The sounds being often used without reference to
any particular occasion, and carrying still their first impressions, they
at last utterly lose their connexion with the particular occasions that
gave rise to them; yet the sound, without any annexed notion, continues to operate as before.[51]

Consequently, whatever effect such words may have on the passions, "they do not derive it from any representation raised in the
mind of the things for which they stand." Burke finds this true
of nonabstract words as well. Words which "form some one determinate composition, as man, horse, tree, castle, &c.,"[52] operate, "not by presenting any image to the mind, but by having
from use the same effect on being mentioned, that their original
has when it is seen."[53]

In the eighteenth century, however, the majority view is that
of Dugald Stewart. Stewart is willing to agree that "a very great
proportion of the words which we habitually employ, have no
effect to 'raise ideas in the mind'; or to excite the powers of conception and imagination."[54] He is convinced, however, that the
primary object of the poet, as distinguished from other writers,
must be to suggest pleasing visual images, and that the pleasure
which the poet conveys "will, in general be found to be propor-
tioned to the beauty and liveliness of the images which he sug-

gests."[55] It is clear that poetry is still in some danger, nearly sixty years after the Richardsons' comments on Milton, of being regarded as a sort of storehouse for getting a fine "Collection of Poetical Pictures."

The poet, writes J. Middleton Murry, "must not allow himself to be corrupted by trying to emulate the art of painting." While many today would agree that nothing is more "wearisome" than "a long passage of pictorial description" in poetry,[56] modern readers may still react favorably to certain passages of allegorical description in eighteenth-century verse. These, however, as I proceed to show in the next chapter, are enlivened by qualities not on the whole characteristic of poetry within the eighteenth-century "tradition of prosopopoeia and allegory."[57]

CHAPTER IV

THE VALUES OF ALLEGORICAL PERSONIFICATION: COLLINS AND GRAY

RACHEL TRICKETT has noticed the importance which eighteenth-century poets attached to "the decorum of a comparison." The poets were

> very conscious [in their allegorical portraits] of the need to choose exactly appropriate illustrations for their ideas, and the ideas themselves very often reflected the bias of the age toward logical inductive reasoning that follows a clear thread of argument.[1]

Miss Trickett finds that

> the allegorical interpretation of mythology which to the Renaissance made the gods and goddesses as real as the nature they represented, had been exchanged [in the eighteenth century] for a more rational appreciation of the appropriateness of the emblem to the attribute, or the single illustration of a clear and isolated philosophical idea.[2]

Joseph Spence's remarks on Spenserian allegory clearly demonstrate the strength of this feeling for emblematic "appropriateness." Spence, it is clear, wished the allegorical figure to illustrate "the appropriate moment, or the isolated and significant single attitude, gesture or incident" which seemed poetically as well as pictorially "to throw into relief the idea, emotion, or theme"[3] which the poet wished to express. Joseph Warton, it will be remembered, praised Lucretius as a "sculptor-poet,"[4] and it is not too much to say that the inner logic of the formal allegorical portrait makes for the production of images which have a certain statuesque quality, especially when allegory is conveyed through a formalized gesture or attitude of body. To attach a heavy weight of symbolic significance to the "single attitude" is, in effect, to throw the allegorical figure into "bold relief," detaching it, as it were, from the background against which it appears. The eighteenth-century poets "were particularly attracted by images of a statuesque effect" because, with these, they "could give the impression of a significant action fixed in a permanent and ideal form."[5] Many of their allegorical figures, accordingly, have a "static" rather than a "mobile" effect.

Several of the figures in Collins's *Ode to the Passions* are of this type. They are presented in "bold relief." The sculpturesque effect is a consequence of the poet's emphasis upon his figures as illustrations of "isolated" ideas. The allegorical significance attached to gesture and movement acts to give an effect of arrested motion: the figures are not allowed to move from the symbolic pedestals to which they are attached. Effects of this sort are a consequence, not as William Gilpin thought, of the poet's copying "forms from the sculptor,"[6] but of the emphasis placed upon the symbolic significance of gesture, motion, or attitude of body.

One of the dangers incident to this mode of allegorical presentation has been noticed by a critic in the *Times Literary Supplement*. Personification, it is said, is "badly used" when, though the figure "comes alive—that is, does something—it does something unworthy or not sufficiently important, either for itself or for the poem."[7] It is questionable whether all the activity ascribed to Collins's figure of Revenge in the *Ode to the Passions* is justified in order to tell us something "characteristic" about this passion. There is a decorum of presentation which must be preserved. If this is violated by an overemphasis on the stage properties or activities of the figure itself, the latent discrepancy between the abstract quality as such and its presumed analogy in sense will be felt as a contradiction, and the figure which embodies this contradiction will, as Johnson said, excite a "conviction of its own absurdity."[8] Collins achieves a much greater success with his figure of Pity than with his figure of Revenge:

> Long, *Pity,* let the Nations view
> Thy sky-worn Robes of tend'rest Blue,
> And Eyes of dewy Light![9]

Pity is vividly pictorialized but she is not presented in "bold re-lief." Collins exercises a poetic restraint which has its reward in the reader's "willing suspension of disbelief." Pity, to be sure, is a conventionally sentimental evocation, but Collins displays a happy talent for pictorial description which raises his figure above the commonplace level of achievement. Most of the allegorical portraits in mid- and late eighteenth-century verse fail to stimulate the relatively "sluggish" allegorical imaginations of modern readers, largely because the great majority of poets who favor this mode of personification do not possess the "fine and sure literary tact"[10] which Collins exercises in his description of Pity.

This literary tact is apparent also in the verse of Thomas Gray, and is responsible for the fact that one or two of his allegorical tableaux still "come alive" for the modern reader. Much of Gray's allegorizing is thoroughly conventional. He shares the mid-century fondness for picturesque allegorical groupings. The fourth stanza of the *Hymn to Adversity* affords a good example of this "catalogue" method of presentation:

> Wisdom in sable garb array'd,
> Immers'd in rapt'rous thought profound,
> And Melancholy, silent maid
> With leaden eye, that loves the ground,
> Still on thy solemn steps attend:
> Warm Charity, the gen'ral friend,
> With Justice, to herself severe,
> And Pity, dropping soft the sadly-pleasing tear.[11]

The abstractions in this passage deserve the criticism which C. V. Deane has made of Gray's personifications in general. Deane finds most of these "pretentiously statuesque."[12] But Gray, like Collins, displays on occasion a poetic tact which gives a more sub-stantial value to his allegorical descriptions.

In *The Progress of Poesy* Gray describes the approach of Cytherea, the goddess of Love:

> Slow melting strains their Queen's approach declare:
> Where'er she turns the Graces homage pay.
> With arms sublime, that float upon the air,
> In gliding state she wins her easy way:
> O'er her warm cheek, and rising bosom, move
> The bloom of young Desire, and purple light of Love.[13]

And in *The Bard* there are the well-known lines:

> Fair laughs the Morn, and soft the Zephyr blows,
> While proudly riding o'er the azure realm
> In gallant trim the gilded Vessel goes;
> Youth on the prow, and Pleasure at the helm;
> Regardless of the sweeping Whirlwind's sway,
> That, hush'd in grim repose, expects his evening-prey.[14]

Earlier in the stanza in which Cytherea appears, Gray had written:

> The rosy-crowned Loves are seen
> On Cytherea's day
> With antic Sports, and blue-eyed Pleasures,
> Frisking light in frolic measures.[15]

This passage might have appeared in almost any of the pseudo-Miltonic odes of the period. A description of the central figure in these odes is normally accompanied by an enumeration of a train of "attendant abstractions."[16] Gray, however, resists the temptation to objectify "young Desire" and "Love" as complete spiritual beings. They are not attendants in the train of Cytherea (as are "antic Sport" and the "blue-eyed Pleasures"), but the very attributes of the goddess herself. These abstractions are frankly metaphorical. They convey something of that effect of pleasurable "surprise" which good metaphor conveys; an effect which acts, in context, to stimulate the visual imagination of the reader so that the passage as a whole seems to recall, as one critic has said, the type of "radiant, florid ceiling painted by Tiepolo."[17]

It is otherwise with the passage on the "gilded Vessel."
"Youth" and "Pleasure" hardly attain the force of metaphor:
they are distinct "persons," similar in this respect to the figures in
the *Hymn to Adversity*. Coleridge, indeed, appears to have regarded these figures as typical instances of Gray's failure to vivify
his abstractions. Coleridge states his preference for the odes of
Collins above those of Gray, and compares the lines on the gilded
vessel unfavorably with Gratiano's lines on the "skarfed bark" in
the *Merchant of Venice:*

> How like a younker or a prodigal,
> The skarfed bark puts from her native bay,
> Hugg'd and embraced by the strumpet wind!
> How like the prodigal doth she return,
> With over-weather'd ribs and ragged sails,
> Lean, rent and beggar'd by the strumpet wind![18]

It is probably true, as J. Shawcross notes, that what Coleridge
blames in Gray is "not so much that he personifies abstractions, as
that he leaves them when personified cold and lifeless; whereas
from Collins they receive a real, not merely a verbal personality."[19] It depends, says Coleridge, "on the compositor's putting,
or not putting, a *small Capital,* both in this, and in many other
passages of the same poet, whether the words should be personifications, or mere abstractions."[20] Coleridge, it would appear,
prefers the realistic particularity of Shakespeare's language as
against Gray's generalized diction: "skarfed bark," with its suggestion of pennants flying, as against "gilded Vessel"; the realism
of the younker-strumpet association as against Gray's euphemis-
tic "Pleasure at the helm"; the vividness of Shakespeare's
"Hugg'd and embraced by the strumpet wind" as against Gray's
"soft the Zephyr blows."

This would be perfectly legitimate criticism of much eighteenth-century poetic practice, but Coleridge has been unfair to
Gray in the present instance because he has not seen the lines on
the gilded vessel for what they really are. The merit of the simile

in Shakespeare arises from the fact that the language enforces a
sense of actuality. We are made to realize, in vivid fashion, the
intensity and violence which accompany the reckless pursuit of
wealth and pleasure, and the equally violent and shattering effects which follow. Gray's lines, on the other hand, are not really
concerned with any particular stratum of human experience.
They are attractive, not because they are an imitation of reality
(although Gray may have intended them as such), but because
they picture a kind of ideal felicity which we are fond of imagining for ourselves in moments of daydream or reverie. The last
two lines, indeed, come as something of an anticlimax; one is
rather inclined to wish the "gilded Vessel" to ride on over the
"azure realm" undisturbed by the "sweeping Whirlwind's
sway." Gray's generalized diction, then, is to be accounted a
happy instance of tact in the choice of language, since a use of
more realistic detail would tend to destroy the effect of the image
as the picture of an ideal (rather than an actual) state of human
felicity.

Gray's lines, according to C. V. Deane, are "sumptuous if superficial allegory, somewhat in the style of an Italian wall-paint-
ing of the High Renaissance."[21] The allegory in this passage and
in that on Cytherea is "superficial," I would suggest, because,
although Gray gives us pleasing pictures, these pictures decorate
rather than animate the verse in which they appear. They have
a "static" rather than a "mobile" effect.

Most allegorical description in eighteenth-century verse is of
this "static" type, but there are a few instances in which allegorical figures take on a more valuable function. This is true, most
notably, of the central figure in Collins's *Ode to Evening*. The
goddess Evening merges with the surrounding landscape; she becomes, in succession, "a country girl, a Fairy Queen, a priestess,
a goddess, a ghost in the sky."[22] She is highly mobile: "by unob-
trusively varying the attributes of his central figure," Collins is
able to portray "evanescent and transitory effects of natural
beauty."[23]

The poetic tact which distinguishes Collins's handling of this figure is displayed again in his treatment of the allegorical figures in the 1746 ode beginning "How sleep the brave." These abstractions are "shadowy forms." They are at once "delicate and majestic."[24] Most allegorical figures in eighteenth-century verse convey a sense of the mental effort which went into their making, but one feels that Collins's "unseen" forms are not so much "created" as "discovered." Lord David Cecil, citing Keats's description of Joy—"Joy, whose hand is ever at his lips/Bidding adieu"—remarks that

the impression we get is that Joy spontaneously embodied itself in a living figure, which flashed unbidden, and as in a vision, before the poet's mental eye.[25]

What Cecil says of Keats's figure may be said also of Collins's "Evening" and of the figures in the 1746 ode, although the word "flashed" implies a kind of abruptness foreign to the quiet and subdued atmosphere of Collins's poems. The poet who is able to convey such an impression has an advantage over the poet whose statuesque figures are ever in some danger of exciting in the reader a conviction of their own absurdity.

One may notice, in this connection, the first stanza from Gray's *Ode on the Pleasure arising from Vicissitude:*

> Now the golden Morn aloft
>   Waves her dew-bespangled wing;
> With vermeil cheek and whisper soft
>   She woo's the tardy spring:
> Till April starts, and calls around
> The sleeping fragrance from the ground;
> And lightly o'er the living scene
> Scatters his freshest, tenderest green.[26]

Gray shows, in this passage, something of that "mythological instinct for personifying properties of nature"[27] which Collins shows in the *Ode to Evening.* It is possible to visualize "the golden morn" and "April" as complete spiritual beings, but they blend so well with the landscape that one is hardly able to detach them from it. They do not draw attention to themselves but to the landscape as a whole, and their effect, as C. V. Deane has said, is to encourage the imagination "to paint the appropriate scene in its own forms and colours."[28] I find no other passage in which Gray so happily blends personification with scenes of natural beauty. The stanza is a momentary triumph of literary taste. Every impulse of the time tended to discourage such an intimate union of the personified abstraction with effects of natural beauty. Even in the *Ode to Evening* Collins somewhat spoils the effect of the poem as a whole by the introduction of "Fancy, Friendship, Science," and "smiling Peace," where, one feels, the shadowy figure of Evening ought still to hold sway, undisturbed by these obtrusive presences.

The effects which Collins achieves in the *Ode to Evening* are not those which most eighteenth-century poets consciously sought to attain, nor do the critics show an appreciation of the poetic values which may result from the skillful intermixture of personification with scenes of natural beauty. Indeed, the factors which acted to establish the prosopopoeia as a statuesque "object of sight" acted also to produce a feeling of irritation in regard to allegorical figures which could not be easily detached from the background, natural or artificial, against which they appeared. James Thomson had written:

> Confessed from yonder slow-extinguished clouds,
> All ether softening, sober Evening takes
> Her wonted station in the middle air,
> A thousand shadows at her beck. First this
> She sends on earth; then that of deeper dye
> Steals soft behind; and then a deeper still,
> In circle following circle, gathers round
> To close the face of things.[29]

"This passage," said John Scott,

blends natural description and personification in a very intricate manner. Both would have been proper, and indeed beautiful, had they been kept asunder. The gradual vanishing or extinction of colour in the clouds, justly discriminates evening, considered as a point of time; but as such vanishing or extinction occasions darkness, it could not possibly render evening visible or perceptible, considered as a person.[30]

Effects of the sort which Collins attains in the *Ode to Evening* run counter to the main lines of eighteenth-century achievement. They remind one of effects attained by the poets of an earlier age when the allegorical interpretation of mythology which had "made the gods and goddesses as real as the nature they represented" had not as yet been exchanged "for a more rational appreciation of the appropriateness of the emblem to the attribute, or the single illustration of a clear and isolated philosophical idea." Personifications of natural phenomena in eighteenth-century verse are, for the most part, symbols of affective states rather than mythological presences. The allegorical figure sums up the meaning which the natural phenomenon has for the poet; it does not become a living presence which is felt to have an existence apart from human life. It is not the least part of Collins's achievement that the intensity of feeling which leads him to see his allegorical abstractions as real persons is accompanied in the *Ode to Evening* by a poetic tact which operates to keep the goddess herself a "shadowy" figure. As a result, we have a poem in which the central figure becomes, not a symbol only of the poet's feelings about evening as a point of time, but a living presence which reveals itself to the vision of the poet as he pierces the veil which separates the world of material reality from the "spirit-world" of the imagination. The goddess Evening "comes alive" because Collins makes one feel that she is not formally, but actually, "a figure of vision." The fact that she is not presented in "bold relief" is a virtue, not a vice, and a virtue not often found in other poems within the eighteenth-century "tradition of prosopopoeia and allegory."

In an article on Collins's verse which appeared in 1923, Alan D. McKillop, finding "romantic intent" in most of Collins's

odes, excepted the *Ode to Evening* as a poem which stood "somewhat apart from the rest of [Collins's] work."[31] Whether or not
the qualities of feeling which I have discerned in this poem are to
be described as "romantic" or as "neoclassic," McKillop was
right in thinking that the poem differed significantly from the
majority of Collins's odes. The *Ode to Evening* has what most of
Collins's odes do not have—near perfection of form, a quality
which is rightly esteemed a virtue of the best neoclassic verse.
This quality is seen elsewhere in the balance and finish of the
Popean couplet, and in the "best Pindaric passages" in Dryden's
odes, where the "streams of words [are] delicately and musically
disposed."[32]

Collins's poem may be compared in this respect to Gray's *Elegy
Written in a Country Church-Yard*. Gray's great achievement in
the *Elegy*

was to crystallize into distinguished expression the conventional
poetizing of the meditative-melancholic line of versifiers who drew
their inspiration so largely from the minor poems of Milton; and he
may be said to have done so by adapting to his ruminative sentiments
and commonplaces an Augustan style.[33]

The "meditative-melancholic" tone which runs through the
Elegy is, as Eleanor Sickles has shown, a marked feature of the
pseudo-Miltonic odes addressed to the goddess Melancholy,[34]
and, it may be added, of many an ode addressed to Contentment,
Solitude, Retirement, and the like. But many of the "ruminative
sentiments and commonplaces" of the *Elegy* are those to which
poets writing in the central neoclassic tradition could give enthusiastic assent, as Johnson's criticism amply demonstrates.[35]

There are, as D. H. Steuert maintains, "two Grays": the Gray

associated with the strong Augustan line, with the Pope of the
Moral Essays and the *Dunciad*, and the Gray of the meditative-melancholic sensibility, closely related to the eighteenth-century Miltonic
school.[36]

Both types of sensibility find expression in the *Elegy*. The *Elegy* is in some respects a great poem in the neoclassic tradition of Pope and Johnson; in others, a poem which gives "distinguished expression" to moods cultivated by the mid-century admirers of *Il Penseroso*. But so far as the manner of treatment is concerned, it is true that Gray, in the *Elegy,* employs "an Augustan style." One notes that Gray uses a type of personification which is suited to the purposes of the contemporary "poetry of statement." The eighth stanza of the *Elegy* reads as follows:

> Let not Ambition mock their useful toil,
> Their homely joys, and destiny obscure;
> Nor Grandeur hear with a disdainful smile,
> The short and simple annals of the poor.[37]

Personification is employed here as a device of rhetoric. It is used to tell us something which does not concern itself. Gray is not interested in telling us something "characteristic" about ambition or grandeur, nor is he interested in the pictorial felicity of these abstractions as elements in the projection of an allegorical "tableau." It is possible to visualize these figures as complete spiritual beings, and it has been seen how the pictorial effects of a similar stanza in the *Elegy* captured the "ready allegorical imagination" of one of Gray's eighteenth-century critics.[38] But the perception of such an effect is incidental to Gray's main purpose. Gray is interested in the rhetorical effect of personification as a mode of statement. Thomas Quayle, who was strongly prejudiced against eighteenth-century "abstractionism," admitted that in this case, the abstractions promote "an economy of expression that is not without dignity and effectiveness, and they thus . . . give an added emphasis to the sentiment."[39] Such a use of personification is evidently to be distinguished from modes of presentation which achieve their purposes, however delicately or subtly, through effects of description. The personifications in the *Elegy* are dramatic rather than pictorial: "They are actors giving up their potential individuality in order to play their part in the life of somebody else."[40] Technically, Gray uses the figure as Pope and Johnson most often use it, but so far as it is employed to give dramatic emphasis to "ruminative sentiments" common to the "line of versifiers who drew their inspiration so largely from the minor poems of Milton," one cannot say that Gray's use of the figure is informed by what F. R. Leavis has called "a positive feeling for the Augustan."[41] This point will be made clearer in Part Two of this study where Johnson's and Pope's use of personification is examined in detail. For the moment I wish only to indicate the chief points of difference between the allegoric and the rhetorical use of personification, and to draw attention to the fact that neither type is good or bad in itself. Each type may have poetic value, although the values of the one will not be the values of the other.

Leaving aside less tangible considerations, it is evident that allegorical description in Collins and Gray is raised above the level of the commonplace by a "fine and sure literary tact" not often displayed by the many mid- and late eighteenth-century poets who favor personification as a "sign" of imaginative "indulgence." This quality reveals itself in the presentation of allegorical figures which are pictorially effective, but not "pretentiously statuesque." And, although this poetic tact or sense of style may not be accompanied, in every instance, by "a positive feeling for the Augustan," it is itself a virtue of the central neoclassic tradition to which Pope belongs rather than of the dissident, pseudo-Miltonic tradition.

Collins and Gray are minor poets compared with Pope, but if the weaker poetic tradition from which they drew so much of their inspiration had produced many poems of the quality of the *Ode to Evening* and the *Elegy Written in a Country Church-Yard,* it would not be possible to say with F. R. Leavis that

the prevailing modes and conventions of the eighteenth-century did not on the whole tend, as those of the seventeenth did, to bring into poetry the vitality of the age.[42]

The next chapter is an illustrative commentary on the truth of
Leavis's statement. The modes and conventions which determine
the use of the personified abstraction in late eighteenth-century
verse result, finally, in the figure's becoming, in Wordsworth's
phrase, "a family language which writers in metre seem to lay
claim to by prescription."[43]

CHAPTER V

ATTITUDES TOWARD PERSONIFICATION
IN THE LATE EIGHTEENTH CENTURY:
DARWIN AND WORDSWORTH

THERE WAS a widespread feeling during the last two decades of
the eighteenth century that poetry had fallen upon evil days. William Hayley called poetry "a declining art,"[1] and T. J. Mathias
found the contemporary literary horizon "perhaps . . . now il-
luminated with its departing beams."[2] The great majority of the
poets most in vogue during the eighties and nineties have not
stood the test of time. The verse of William Hayley, Erasmus
Darwin, Anna Seward, Mary Robinson, Hannah Cowley, and
many others is now forgotten except by students. W. J. Courthope believes this due to the overrefinement of the age. The
popular poets of the time forgot that

the true spirit of classical poetry was not to be found in mere forms—
whether the impersonations of Darwin or the drivelling affectations
of the Cruscans—but in the energetic expression of civic ideas.[3]

However this may be, it is at least certain that the neoclassic tradition no longer enjoyed the authority it once possessed. There was
a new spirit in the air, but until the formulation of romantic doctrine in the prose and poetry of Wordsworth and Coleridge, there
was no certain indication of what this new spirit would mean for
poetry.

Meanwhile, the poets pursued novelty in their attempts to
engage the attention of a public tired of the old themes and
methods of treatment. Hayley, in his immensely popular *Tri-*

umphs of Temper (1781), tried to lend his poem "an air of novelty" by the use of various devices, including the employment of "real and . . . visionary scenes . . . in alternate cantos."[4] The Della Cruscans enjoyed a brief moment of popularity before William Gifford explained to a bemused public that the lavish use of the farfetched conceit and the wildly scrambled metaphor was not evidence, necessarily, of tender sentiment or of genuine poetry.[5] The greatest popular success of the period, however, was Erasmus Darwin's *Botanic Garden.* Darwin's ambitious attempt to unite poetry with science achieved a popularity which lasted well into the following century. It was not until 1809 that Byron was able to notice the neglect of the *Botanic Garden* as "some proof of returning taste," and there were serious attempts to follow in the Darwinian path as late as 1828.[6] "Wordsworth's famous essay on poetic diction," writes Frederick Pottle, "is from beginning to end an anxious attack on the poetry of Erasmus Darwin, then much more popular than his own."[7] The 1800 preface to the *Lyrical Ballads* is an "anxious attack," not only on the verse of Erasmus Darwin, but on the whole theory of poetry which lies behind the verse. The preface is of great importance for the purposes of this book. Wordsworth tells us why the romantic poets rejected the personified abstraction as employed in late eighteenth-century verse. It is evident at once that the rejection is based upon a view of poetry radically different from that entertained by the popular poets of the eighties and nineties. Darwin is singled out for attack because the *Botanic Garden* is, in 1800, the best-known example of the kind of poetry which Wordsworth deplores.

The *Botanic Garden,* however, is not an isolated *tour de force.* The view of poetry which informs it is grounded in the critical theory of the past. This view has its origins in that strain of critical theory which, receiving its most important formulation in the critical essays of Addison, finds later expression in the verse of the Wartons, Collins, and many lesser mid-century poets. The tendency to identify pictorial imagery with the very

essence of poetry itself was, as has been seen, a prominent element in this strain of critical theory. One remembers Addison's
dictum concerning the importance of "Beautiful descriptions
and images" as constituting the "life and spirit of Poetry."[8] The
prosopopoeia, as I have shown, is to be included in the category
of those images which effect their purposes through an appeal to
the picture-receiving faculty of mind. Personification, moreover,
was especially favored as a peculiarly poetic figure of speech
since it was associated in the minds of eighteenth-century poets
and critics with the higher levels of imaginative activity.

As the century proceeded, the "understanding" lost its key
position in eighteenth-century poetics, to be replaced by imagination-fancy. The decline of the neoclassic critical ethos was accompanied by an increasing emphasis upon those uses of language which were believed to separate the productions of the
imagination from those of the understanding. The distinction
which Addison had made between poetry and prose "fiction" as
products of the former, and intellectual or argumentative prose
as a product of the latter, was extended by Joseph Warton to
include an opposition between the mid-century lyric and the
earlier neoclassic poetry of statement. The lyric was favored because it was thought to appeal to the imagination rather than to
the understanding, and so was far more "poetic" than didactic
or satiric genres. The essential distinction, however, lay, not between one form or genre as opposed to others, but between what
were considered the "prosaic" elements in verse and what was
variously termed "pure poetry" or "the most poetical poetry,"
wherever this might be found.[9] There are readers of poetry,
wrote William Whitehead in 1762, who, "mistaking prejudice
for taste,"

> . . . on one species all their rapture waste.
> Tho', various as the flowers which paint the year,
> In rainbow charms the changeful Nine appear,
> The different beauties coyly they admit,
> And to one standard would confine our wit.

> Some MANNER'D VERSE delights; while some can raise
> To fairy FICTION their exstatic gaze,
> Admire PURE POETRY, and revel there
> On sightless forms, and pictures of the air![10]

R. H. Bowers asks what Whitehead means by the phrase "pure poetry." F. A. Pottle replies that " 'pure poetry' is perhaps like 'pure mathematics'—totally divorced from any practical application."[11] This is true enough, but Whitehead's phrase has a much more definite meaning. Whitehead is thinking of the fairy way of writing. He is thinking of that type of deviation from literal language which involves "the poetic creation of another world, peopled with its own manner of non-empirical beings."[12] Whitehead, it should be noted, does not think of "PURE POETRY" as inherently more valuable than "MANNER'D VERSE." He professes to admire both kinds, and urges the desirability of a catholic taste. One should at least be tolerant: "what each thinks the test/Let each enjoy: but not condemn the rest."[13] Others, however, agreed with Joseph Warton that "the 'true Poet' and writer of 'PURE POETRY' is stamped solely by 'a creative and glowing IMAGINATION,' "[14] and that pure poetry is inherently more valuable than any other type. Personification appears as a prominent element in such poetry because it was regarded as "one of the greatest efforts . . . of a warm and lively imagination."[15] The identification of pure poetry with personification is made explicit by Mrs. Barbauld in the preface to her edition of Collins. Mrs. Barbauld divides poetry into two classes. The first class includes didactic, descriptive, and dramatic poetry: everything, in short, except "what may be called pure Poetry, or Poetry in the abstract." Pure poetry "is conversant with an imaginary world, peopled with beings of its own creation. It deals in splendid imagery, bold fiction, and allegorical personages." "All that is properly *Lyric Poetry*" is "pure poetry."[16]

Although associated especially with the lyric, the prosopopoeia is a prominent feature also in the didactic and philosophical poems of the late eighteenth century. While the content of the lengthy didactic or philosophical poem was often felt to be essentially unpoetic since, as Vicesimus Knox said, the "information" which the poem contained might "be conveyed in prose,"[17] an extensive use of the type of imagery which appeared in the lyric would act to raise the poet's verse to the level of "poetry." "Verse" for Anna Seward was simply "prosaic" content delivered in metre. It was

> in its very nature, artful; though, what should be its essence, poetry, that is, the metaphors, allusions, and imagery, are the natural product of a glowing and raised imagination. There may be verse without poetry, and poetry without verse; but when the genuine bard assumes these fetters, which custom has prescribed him, surely no elegance, no ornament, is beneath his care, which may contribute to embellish them.[18]

An extensive use of the prosopopoeia would of itself act to raise the didactic poet's verse to the level of "poetry," since, as John Aikin said, the "bold prosopopoeia" makes one of those figures "supposed *of themselves* to constitute poetry."[19] The didactic or philosophical poet could achieve through extensive personification something of that imaginative splendor which the lyric poet sought to attain through the creation of a whole world of "allegorical personages."

Such a theory of poetry contains the seeds of its own destruction. Its proponents tend to see "poetic personification, together with the fairy way of writing," as "the highest achievement of poetic imagination."[20] But whatever the situation with regard to poetry, it is the "prosaic" understanding rather than the poetic imagination which remains throughout the eighteenth century the most important of all human faculties. "Pure poetry" might be the product, exclusively, of imagination-fancy, but if so, it could never become much more than an amusement, since "poetic personification" and "the fairy way of writing" were

commonly regarded as having little if any connection with the
activities of men "as enjoying and suffering beings."[21]

Johnson once repeated the "common remark" that, "as there is
no necessity for our having poetry at all, it being merely a luxury,
an instrument of pleasure, it can have no value, unless when
exquisite in its kind."[22] Poetry might be a luxury but Johnson
could give it a more substantial place in the total scheme of things
than Mrs. Barbauld or Anna Seward, since Johnson believed
true poetry a product of "reason" as well as imagination. Great
poetry had for Johnson the dignity which attached in the eighteenth century to any activity which could be said to proceed from
the exercise of the rational faculty. But the late eighteenth-century conception of imagination-fancy was not of sufficient weight
to support a like degree of faith in the substantial character of
its productions. Mrs. Barbauld admired the poetry of William
Collins, but she believed such poetry could never be popular
since it demanded a far higher degree of taste in the reader
than could ordinarily be expected, and since there was not
enough "story" or other paraphrasable content.[23] In spite of
her admiration for Collins, Mrs. Barbauld would, in effect, hand
over the odes of Collins and "all that is properly *Lyric Poetry*"
to become the exclusive property of the connoisseur. And so it
seems that the "purer" the poetry, the more it conforms to its
ideal state as the product, exclusively, of imagination-fancy, the
less real influence it will have in the life of the community at
large. And this is true because the function of imagination is
assumed to be the presentation of "bold fiction"; the "purer" the
poetry, the further removed from empirical reality the phenomena with which it deals. Pure poetry, then, cannot be expected
to hold much appeal for readers who turn to poetry expecting
to find images of "man and nature."[24] It is no wonder that
Wordsworth protested, or that Coleridge sought to replace this
conception with one more favorable to poetry as an art which
"brings the whole soul of man into activity."[25] That atmosphere of unreality which Mrs. Barbauld associates with the em-

ployment of "allegorical personages" in poetry is just what Wordsworth is most anxious to avoid: personified abstractions are banished because "I have wished to keep the Reader in the company of flesh and blood, persuaded that by so doing I shall interest him."[26] The condemnation of the figure is a part of Wordsworth's general condemnation of anything which detracts from the character of the poet as one who deals with "the general passions and thoughts and feelings of men."[27]

There is irony in the fact that Wordsworth's remarks are directed against a kind of poetic endeavor which mirrors the shift from a neoclassic to a romantic theory of art. Poets and critics, influenced by the classical theory of rhetoric, had tended to regard the poem as a piece of persuasive discourse. They agreed with Horace that the poet's aim is to blend profit with pleasure, "at once delighting and instructing the reader."[28] This "pragmatic orientation" stresses the relation of the work of art to the audience; gradually, however, during the eighteenth century, the audience recedes into the background, "giving place to the poet himself and his own mental powers and emotional needs, as the predominant cause and even the end and the test of art."[29] Addison and many of the poets and critics discussed in chapter II of this book may be viewed as moving away from the pragmatic theory toward what becomes, in Wordsworth, an "expressive" theory of art. The value attached to "pure poetry" as a product of the poet's "original invention"—of his own vehement feelings and "flights of fancy"—may be seen as a step in the direction of Wordsworth's view of poetry as "the spontaneous overflow of powerful feelings."[30]

A general consequence is that the language of the poet—the specific quality of his diction—becomes increasingly important. Anna Seward and William Wordsworth are both deeply concerned with poetic diction, since, if true poetry is the expression, either of the "powerful feelings" of the poet, or a product of his "glowing and raised imagination," it follows that

of the elements constituting a poem, the element of diction, especially figures of speech, becomes primary; and the burning question
is, whether these are the natural utterance of emotion and imagination or the deliberate aping of poetic conventions.[31]

Wordsworth, of course, saw in personification as employed in the
verse of his contemporaries, the "deliberate aping" of a poetic
convention, but the preface to the *Lyrical Ballads* is, from the
point of view of the literary historian, simply another in a series
of attempts which were being made to answer the question:
"What kind of language is truly the language of feeling and/or
imagination?" I have discussed the factors which tended to
establish the personified abstraction as an important element in
such language. One may add that Erasmus Darwin's attitude
toward the figure is, like that of Wordsworth, the product of "a
carefully conceived theory of poetry";[32] a theory, moreover,
which attempts an answer to the same question which Wordsworth set himself to resolve in the preface to the *Lyrical Ballads*.
The fact that Wordsworth's answer is very different from that
of Darwin is a measure of the former poet's romanticism; the
fact that he and Darwin are concerned with the same problem is
evidence of Wordsworth's position in a line of descent which
takes one back through the Wartons and Collins to Addison and
his papers on the pleasures of imagination.

It should not be supposed, however, that there was entire
satisfaction, prior to the time of Wordsworth, with the kind of
language employed in the poems of those who wished to "indulge" their imaginations. The unfortunate results which attended the efforts of lesser mid-century poets to write verse
which should attain the status of "pure poetry" were noticed
long before 1800. In 1777, there appeared a satirical poem entitled *Bagley* by Alexander Schomberg, inscribed "To the Authors of Elegies, Visions, Legendary Tales, and Allegorical
Poems, the great Assertors of true Poetry in the present Age."[33]
Schomberg's poem satirizes the principal "beauties" observable

in this poetry. These are "its elevation and grandeur of expression; its bold and animated metaphors"; and "the use of the Prosopopaea."[34] Selecting his instances from "two or three of the chief Poets," Schomberg attacks the use of the prosopopoeia in the verse, chiefly, of John Ogilvie, William Mason, and John Langhorne. Ogilvie, the most ardent mid-century proponent of personification, is the principal butt. Schomberg fully shares the contemporary attitude which saw in personification a sign of the imaginative sublime. He criticizes the moderns

not for the mere *use* of this figure (for even the frigid Ancients used it *sometimes* . . . but for that *constant* study of giving life to *every* object and idea, and of throwing . . . on the most trifling circumstance, with the assistance of grand and elevated language, the majesty of the most important.[35]

The moderns degrade the inherent sublimity of the figure by applying it indiscriminately to objects and ideas which are trivial in themselves. Schomberg's criticism is in accordance with the facts. Ogilvie, who said that "frequent personifications . . . are the criterions by which we estimate the genius of the Poet," believed himself (with some reason) the first critic to have discussed personification in any detail.[36] His *Providence* (1764) and his *Britannia* (1801) were written in the belief that the use of figures, and especially the frequent use of the personified abstraction, remained "the essential characteristic whereby the work of a Poet is distinguished from the plain narration of an Historian."[37] Both poems are filled with personified abstractions, not all of which (to be fair) achieve the degree of pretentious ineptitude displayed in the following lines:

> Tell why the hand
> Of strutting Impudence, unlicens'd, grasps
> The palm of worth, and his indignant brow
> Looks down, while meek-ey'd Modesty dismay'd
> Mantles her cheek in crimson, and retires
> To blush in Silence![38]

For minor poets like Ogilvie, the frequent introduction of personified abstractions was a sign that they too were possessed of
the true poetic fire, however noticeable their deficiencies in other
respects. No one, at least, could accuse them of writing prose
instead of poetry so long as they made it their business to give
"life to *every* object and idea." To personify served notice that
one was being "poetic."

An overemphasis on devices of style usually accompanies periods of poetic impoverishment. The latter decades of the eighteenth century were no exception. Ogilvie treats the theme of
divine providence allegorically in the belief that this manner of
treatment is inherently more poetic than others. Darwin personifies the vegetable kingdom in the belief that he is making
poetry out of "the System of Linneus."[39]

Erasmus Darwin's *Loves of the Plants* appeared in 1789, followed two years later by *The Economy of Vegetation,* the two
together comprising *The Botanic Garden.* According to Anna
Seward, Darwin, on seeing a poem of hers, suggested that she
versify the system of Linnaeus since this was unexplored poetic
ground. Her task would be to transform plants and flowers into
human beings, thereby reversing the procedure of Ovid in the
Metamorphoses. She tells us that she persuaded Darwin to un-
dertake the work himself.[40] We have, accordingly, a poem in
which "universal personification [is] the order of the Muse
. . . not to be infringed."[41] But personification "is a device of
art, not the product of art." It is not good or bad in itself; its
esthetic value depends upon its organic relation to the context in
which it appears.[42] Darwin's use of personification is artificial
because he ignores this truth. As in Ogilvie's *Providence,* personification becomes "the product of art." It is mechanically introduced according to a prearranged formula.

Darwin's theory of poetry is in the tradition of Addison and
the Wartons. For Darwin the principal distinction between
prose and poetry lies in the fact that "poetry admits of but few

words expressive of very abstracted ideas, whereas prose abounds with them." Like Addison, he emphasizes the picture-making function of poetry:

As our ideas derived from visible objects are more distinct than those derived from the objects of our other senses, the words expressive of these ideas belonging to vision make up the principal part of poetic language. That is, the poet writes principally to the eye; the prose writer uses more abstracted terms.

Darwin believed that "personifications and allegories distinguish poetry," and, like the Wartons and Richard Hurd, he emphasized the pictorial qualities of such figures: personifications and allegories "are other arts of bringing objects before the eye; or of expressing sentiments in the language of vision."[43]

The growing interest in picturesque landscape fostered by poems such as Mason's *English Garden* and by the various "tours" of William Gilpin may have confirmed Darwin in the belief that a devotion to picture in poetry would prove acceptable to the public. It must be said, however, that a comparison of the notes to the *Botanic Garden* with those appended to his later poem, *The Temple of Nature,* shows that Darwin had not, in the former poem, evolved any specialized theory of the picturesque such as those propagated by Mason and Gilpin. The word "picturesque," as Darwin uses it, is sometimes merely a synonym for "visible"; at other times it refers generally to any poetic image which exhibits "the obvious characteristics of visual art." Darwin does not, like Gilpin, associate the term with special qualities or appearances such as roughness, grotesqueness, varied surfaces, and the like.[44] It is clear that the emphasis on pictorial effects in the *Botanic Garden* is a result, chiefly, of Darwin's theory of poetic imagination, a theory which holds that the poet "must create visual images" since the language of poetry "must never be as abstract as the language of prose."[45] If the images in the *Botanic Garden* display the obvious characteristics of visual art, this is due to Darwin's belief in the validity of the poetry-painting parallel rather than to a preference for particular qualities in objects which supposedly rendered them especially suitable for painting.[46] Darwin asked himself the question:

How can one write a poem on scientific processes and be pictorial and not abstract? Allegory, personification, and simile is the only answer. Everything must be interpreted through symbols, if fantastic none the less concrete. If no concrete symbol can be found, then the abstraction must be addressed directly, hailed by name and importuned, and thus dragged bodily before the mind of the reader. With Darwin these figures of speech are not mere idle ornamentation; they are the expression of his carefully conceived theory of poetry.[47]

As a consequence, every passage in the *Botanic Garden* is as picturesque (in the nontechnical sense of the term) as Darwin can make it. In the descriptive passages natural phenomena are personified as a matter of course; in passages of "sentiment" personified abstractions are employed to achieve similar picturesque effects, as in this digression on slavery:

> Hark! heard ye not that piercing cry,
> Which shook the waves and rent the sky?—
> E'en now, e'en now, on yonder Western shores
> Weeps pale Despair, and writhing Anguish roars:
> E'en now in Afric's groves with hideous yell
> Fierce Slavery stalks, and slips the dogs of hell.[48]

What Anna Seward called Darwin's "too exclusive devotion to distinct picture in poetry" is evident throughout the poem.[49] A striking example is afforded by the lines personifying the "moments":

> While each light *Moment,* as it dances by
> With feathery foot and pleasure-twinkling eye,
> Feeds from its baby-hand, with many a kiss,
> The callow nestlings of domestic bliss.[50]

This was too much even for Miss Seward, one of Darwin's staunch admirers. "The moments," she says, "become unpleasing from being too distinctly described, with their kisses and their baby hands."[51]

The truth is that Darwin, like Collins, takes seriously certain of the critical precepts popular in his own day. He does not question the validity of the poetry-painting parallel any more than Collins questioned the view which saw the poetic imagination as a faculty devoted to the evocation of "unreal" scenes. Collins was at least partially successful because he was a poet; Darwin is much less so because he is first of all a man of science. Darwin is not really interested in poetry for its own sake; he versifies science only because he believes the best way of introducing the public to "the knowledge of Botany" is by leading the votaries of imagination "from the looser analogies, which dress out the imagery of poetry, to the stricter ones, which form the ratiocination of philosophy."[52] Darwin thinks of poetry as a means of popularizing science, nor does he think of it as a serious pursuit, comparable in dignity and importance with science. The bookseller in the "First Interlude" asks if the office of poetry is "only to amuse?" Darwin replies that

the muses are young ladies; we expect to see them dressed; though not like some modern beauties, with so much gauze and feather, that "the lady herself is the least part of her." There are, however, didactic pieces of poetry, which are much admired, as the Georgics of Virgil, Mason's English Garden, Hayley's Epistles; nevertheless science is best delivered in prose, as its mode of reasoning is from stricter analogies than metaphors or similes.[53]

By and large, it would seem that the office of poetry is "only to amuse." It would be false to say that poetry was regarded as one of the lesser arts by late eighteenth-century men of letters, but they most certainly did not approach it in a spirit of high seriousness,[54] a fact which provoked Wordsworth's ire. Wordsworth was indignant with those

who talk of Poetry, as of a matter of amusement and idle pleasure; who will converse with us as gravely about a *taste* for Poetry, as they express it, as if it were a thing as indifferent as a taste for rope-dancing, or Frontiniac or Sherry.[55]

Darwin's complacency in this respect is a natural consequence of the prevailing tendency to identify the essence of poetry with a particular mode of expression. Darwin and his contemporaries mistook the "ornaments" of poetry for its substance. Wordsworth saw this clearly enough. One of the principal aims of the 1800 preface is to show that true poetry is something more than a source of amusement, and that the pleasure it affords is "of a purer, more lasting, and more exquisite nature"[56] than was easily conceivable by those laboring under popular misconceptions concerning the nature and purposes of the poet's art. These misconceptions seemingly worked to exalt the nature of the poet's art by effecting a number of formal distinctions between the language of poetry and "lesser" forms of discourse. But Wordsworth saw these distinctions as a degrading force since they tended to make people think of poetry as a thing apart: a form of artistic endeavor which might or might not be of interest to one. These distinctions defined poetry according to its external appearances; they established it as a fine art for which one might or might not develop a *taste*.

But, for Wordsworth, true poetry was "the image of man and nature."[57] It was of vital importance, not merely to connoisseurs, but to men everywhere. The poet, accordingly, must think and feel "in the spirit of human passions." How then, Wordsworth asks, can the language of the poet "differ in any material degree from that of all other men who feel vividly and see clearly"? The poet "must express himself as other men express themselves"; he must avoid the language of other poets or of men like himself, if such language fails to reflect the speech of the people as a whole.[58] It follows that the distinctions commonly drawn between the language of poetry and the language of prose are false. The true distinction is between "Poetry and Matter of Fact, or Science."[59] The poet and the man of science both seek truth, but

the Man of science seeks truth as a remote and unknown benefactor; he cherishes and loves it in his solitude: the Poet, singing a song in which all human beings join with him, rejoices in the presence of truth as our visible friend and hourly companion.[60]

In other words, the poet deals with subjects which are of interest to all men, whereas the man of science, as a discoverer, deals with truths which are necessarily remote from the common interests of humanity. Hence the basis for Wordsworth's attack on Darwin. Botany is not a proper subject for poetry because most men are unfamiliar with the objects and relations which it contemplates, and consequently can be little affected, "as enjoying and suffering beings," by what the poet has to say of these.[61] On the other hand,

if the labours of Men of science should ever create any material revolution, direct or indirect, in our condition, and in the impressions we habitually receive, the Poet will sleep no more than at present; he will be ready to follow the steps of the Man of science . . . carrying sensation into the midst of the objects of the science itself. The remotest discoveries of the Chemist, the Botanist, or Mineralogist, will be as proper objects of the Poet's art as any upon which it can be employed, if the time should ever come when these things shall be familiar to us, and the relations under which they are contemplated by the followers of these respective sciences shall be manifestly and palpably material to us as enjoying and suffering beings. If the time should ever come when what is now called science, thus familiarized to men, shall be ready to put on, as it were, a form of flesh and blood, the Poet will lend his divine spirit to aid the transfiguration, and will welcome the Being thus produced, as a dear and genuine inmate of the household of man.

The remotest discoveries of science will then be objects of universal interest and the proper subjects of the poet's art. The poet will then be under no incentive to "break in upon the sanctity and truth of his pictures by transitory and accidental ornaments"—as Darwin does—endeavoring thereby "to excite admiration of himself by arts, the necessity of which must manifestly depend upon the assumed meanness of his subject."[62]

Of these transitory and accidental ornaments, the personified abstraction, as the most prominent of all at the time when Words-

worth wrote, is singled out for particular mention. It is condemned because it does not make "any natural or regular part" of
the language really used by men. Wordsworth does not, any more
than Schomberg, reject the personified abstraction as bad in itself: it is a "figure of speech occasionally prompted by passion,"
and he claims to have made use of it as such in the *Lyrical Ballads*.
But, like Schomberg, Wordsworth sees that the personified abstraction has become "a mechanical device of style." It had become "a family language which Writers in metre seem to lay
claim to by prescription."[63]

The body of poetic theory which has been examined in these
chapters had unfortunate results so far as the history of eighteenth-century personification is concerned. If the discussion were
concluded at this point, few would be inclined to quarrel with
Wordsworth's general condemnation of the figure. With very
few exceptions, the allegorical personification in eighteenth-century verse is not of sufficient poetic value to justify the claims
made for it as one of the highest achievements of poetic imagination. The occasional successes noted in chapter IV do not out-
weigh the many failures.

The shortcomings of the theory itself are sufficiently evident.
The overemphasis on the personified abstraction as a peculiarly
poetic device of style is a measure of the weakness inherent in a
critical tradition which is unable to arrive at a satisfactory insight
into the essential nature of poetic imagination. The misuse of
personification stems from its association with an unsatisfactory
"picture-making" concept of imagination, an association which
leads to the near identification of the prosopopoeia with the "essence" of poetry itself. "Poetry" is identified with particular effects of language rather than with the total contents of the poem,
and it is this which gives rise, in a period of poetic decline, to the
use of personification as "a mechanical device of style."

But the weaknesses of the allegorical type of personification
are best seen when this use of the figure is contrasted with instances in which it is employed as a device of rhetoric. When

Wordsworth said that he rejected the personified abstraction because he wished to keep his readers in the company of "flesh and
blood," he struck at the heart of current theory. The personified
abstraction was valued by Wordsworth's contemporaries precisely because it was thought of as a "nonempirical being" in-
habiting regions of fancy far removed from the world of visible
reality. But, for Wordsworth, the true personification was not an
unreal object from an imaginary world but a purely rhetorical
figure "prompted" by human passion. It had to do with the feelings and affections of men and women in real life. It was of value
only insofar as it seemed to provide appropriate expression, in
language, for emotions arising out of one's contact with the actualities of life. For Wordsworth, true personification was a figure of rhetoric rather than a figure of fancy, and in spite of his
general condemnation of the figure, the best eighteenth-century
poets will be found to employ the figure effectively as a device of
rhetoric. It is this use of the figure which forms the subject of discussion in Part Two of this study.

Part Two

CHAPTER VI

PERSONIFICATION AS A FIGURE
OF RHETORIC: JOHNSON

IN PART ONE I discussed a type of eighteenth-century personification which was intended to make a strong appeal to the sense of sight. A distinction was made in chapter V between this type of personification and the type which Gray employs in the *Elegy Written in a Country Church-Yard*. As used in the *Elegy*, personification was found to enhance the value of statement in poetry by giving dramatic emphasis to the idea or sentiment which the poet was concerned to express. It was maintained, however, that Gray's use of the figure in the *Elegy* did not, in every instance, reflect a "positive feeling for the Augustan." This part of the book deals with poets whose best verse more fully and more adequately reflects the varied elements of strength which belong to the Augustan tradition in eighteenth-century verse.

The theory of poetic imagination examined in chapter V was criticized because it led poets and their readers to place too much emphasis on the image-making faculty. The views of the major Augustan poets are nearer to the modern concept of poetic imagination as a faculty which involves an effort of the total mind. No attempt is made in these chapters at a comprehensive definition of the term "imagination." To say that imagination involves an effort of the total mind is only to recognize the inadequacy of eighteenth-century "mechanical" or "divisive" theories of mental operations. While it is maintained in the following chapters that the use of the prosopopoeia in certain poems of Pope and

Johnson is "imaginative" in the modern sense of the term, what is meant is that their use of the figure attains certain values—not necessarily *every* value—which modern readers expect from imagery in general, and from metaphor in particular.

Dryden is one of the first critics to give a definition of the creative process which is at all adequate to express a modern view of this activity. According to Dryden,

The first happiness of the poet's imagination is properly invention, or finding of the thought; the second is fancy, or the variation, deriving, or moulding, of that thought, as the judgment represents it proper to the subject; the third is elocution, or the art of clothing and adorning that thought, so found and varied, in apt, significant, and sounding words: the quickness of the imagination is seen in the invention, the fertility in the fancy, and the accuracy in the expression.[1]

As T. S. Eliot has said, "for Dryden 'imagination' was the whole process of poetic creation in which fancy was one element."[2] The poetic imagination is thus a many-sided faculty. It includes the invention, fancy, and judgment that go to the making of a poem. A recent critic has called Dryden's conception "new" and "comprehensive."[3] It held, indeed, much promise for the future, but this promise was not followed up by Addison. Addison was concerned primarily with the visual imagination. This led him to place an undue emphasis upon the importance of picturesque imagery in poetry, an attitude which must be said to represent "a retrogression from Dryden's insight."[4]

While the views of Pope and Johnson on the character of the poetic imagination are similar in certain respects to those of Addison, these critics place much less emphasis upon the visual imagination. In a letter to Swift, Pope shows what he means by the term "imagination." He envies Swift the freedom of invention allowed by such a work as *Gulliver's Travels*. His own poems allowed him no such latitude:

My system is a short one, and my circle narrow. Imagination has no limits, and that is a sphere in which you may move on to eternity;

but where one is confined to truth, or, to speak more like a human creature, to the appearances of truth, we soon find the shortness of our tether.[5]

Like Addison, Pope equates the imagination with the unreal; it is opposed to truth which deals with realities, and the poet who deals with such realities exercises, not imagination, but reason or understanding, the faculty which enables us to discover truth. In the long run, it is the poetry of "truth and sentiment" which Pope consistently favors. In the "advertisement" to the *Epistle to Arbuthnot,* Pope writes: "If [the epistle] have any thing pleasing, it will be That by which I am most desirous to please, the *Truth* and the *Sentiment."*[6] As Geoffrey Tillotson says, "by truth Pope meant fact, the actualities of the life around him."[7] Austin Warren has shown how Pope, in his edition of Shakespeare, emphasizes Shakespeare's common sense, the true-to-life nature of his characters, and the element of "gnomic wisdom" in his poetry.[8]

If Pope accepts the Addisonian equation of the imagination with the unreal, he places much less emphasis upon the picture-making function of imagination-fancy. In the preface to the translation of the *Iliad,* Pope praises Homer's invention. This term is opposed to judgment throughout and is sometimes equated with fancy. It is responsible, however, for Homer's marvellous insight into the "inward Passions and Affections" of men, as well as for his skill in describing the "outward Forms and Images of Things."[9] It is in his criticism of Homer that Pope comes nearest to the modern view of imaginative creation as an effort of the total mind. Invention is opposed to judgment throughout Pope's criticism of the *Iliad,* since Pope is concerned primarily with pointing out, not what Homer has in common with other poets, but in what he surpasses them. He is careful to point out, however, that one is not to think that

Homer wanted Judgment, because *Virgil* had it in a more eminent degree; or that *Virgil* wanted Invention, because *Homer* possesst a larger share of it: Each of these great Authors had more of both than perhaps any Man besides, and are only said to have less in Comparison with each one another.[10]

Pope's conception of the terms "Invention" and "Judgment" is comprehensive. Homer, he says,

in his lowest narrations or speeches, is ever easy, flowing, copious, clear, and harmonious. He shows not less *Invention,* in assembling the humbler, than the greater, thoughts and images; nor less *Judgment* in proportioning the style and the versification to these, than to the other. Let it be remembered, that the same genius that soared the highest, and from whom the greatest models of the *Sublime* are derived, was also he who stooped the lowest, and gave to the simple Narrative its utmost perfection.[11]

Nearly every quality of mind that Dryden included in his definition of the poetic imagination is included here by implication under the general terms *"Invention"* and *"Judgment."* True poetic genius, for Pope as for Dryden, is an expression of the total mind.

Samuel Johnson

defined *imagination* as "Fancy; the power of forming ideal pictures; the power of representing things absent to one's self or others." He defined *fancy* as "Imagination; the power by which the mind forms to itself images and representations of things, persons, or scenes of being."[12]

This conception is thoroughly Addisonian in that it emphasizes the picture-making function of mind, but, as J. H. Hagstrum points out, "a theoretical statement does not explain Johnson's paradoxical practice." In praising and censuring the imagination, Johnson "seems to have found the faculty to be considerably more powerful for good or evil than its position in empirical epistemology seems to suggest."[13] From one point of view, the imagination was regarded by Johnson as simply the image-making faculty—it was, in James Beattie's words, "that power which combines ideas into new forms or assemblages." It was not this quality of imagination which impressed Johnson as powerful for good or evil. But the imagination was also "that power of mind

which contemplates *ideas* (that is, *thoughts* or *notions*) without
referring them to real existence, or to past experience," and it was
this quality of imagination which Johnson "feared, censured and
attempted to bridle." He feared that power of imagination which
evokes the "fanciful" and the "visionary," that is, whatever had
no solid foundation in the world of empirical reality, but was
"bred only in the imagination."[14] Johnson's fear of insanity may
have been a factor in his distrust of the "fictional" quality which
adhered to the contemporary conception of imagination-fancy.
"All power of fancy over reason," he said, "is a degree of insanity."[15] Hagstrum finds his attitude toward the imagination "a
combination of fascination and fear."[16]

Johnson's distrust of the imagination led him to emphasize the
element of thought in all great poetry, but it did not bar him from
recognizing the imagination as a "fervid and active" quality,
necessarily present in any act of true poetic creation. Hagstrum
calls attention to the quality of language in Johnson's description
of the activity of mind which went into the creation of *Paradise
Lost:*

The thoughts which are occasionally called forth . . . are such as
could only be produced by an imagination in the highest degree
fervid and active, to which materials were supplied by incessant
study and unlimited curiosity. The heat of Milton's mind may be
said to sublimate his learning, to throw off into his work the spirit
of science, unmingled with its grosser parts.[17]

Thus does Johnson's very language "leap from one psychological
category to another, from reason to fancy, from imagination to
thought, across the boundaries artificially set up by neoclassical
criticism."[18] Like Dryden and Pope, Johnson perceives that
poetic genius is "the heightened power of all the faculties of the
mind cooperating to produce excellence."[19]

Much of the poetry of Joseph Warton and practically all the
poetry of William Collins is written with the conviction in mind
that true poetry is the product, ideally, of only one faculty of
mind—imagination-fancy—and it has been seen how their con-

ception of this faculty as one which pictures "a world of ideal forms" determined the type of personification employed in their poetry. I am now to consider how this figure is employed by men who think of true poetry as a product of all the major faculties of mind acting in combination, so to speak. Reason is "practical reason" for Pope and Johnson. They value it as a guide to conduct. Interest is focused upon reason in its relation to problems of human behavior, and the poet, as well as the philosopher, is expected to deal significantly with these problems. In Pope and Johnson, therefore, personification is employed by men who consider true poetry the product of a mind actively engaged in giving significant expression to the "actualities of life."

The poetry of Pope and Johnson has risen steadily in public estimation within the last twenty years. As George Sherburn has said, one of the difficulties to the appreciation of Pope during the nineteenth century lay in the failure of the reading public "to regard as aesthetic, poetry that grows from enthusiasm for abstract truths rather than from some emotion derived from experience of life at first hand."[20] But

the discovery of moral aphorisms concealed in verse is far less distressing today than it was before the arrival of poetry written by—to name three dissimilar poets—Thomas Hardy, E. A. Robinson, and Mr. T. S. Eliot.[21]

Aphoristic statement in poetry makes for "abstractionism" if not for personification in the fullest sense of the word. Johnson's celebrated lines are an example:

> This mournful truth is ev'ry where confess'd,
> SLOW RISES WORTH, BY POVERTY DEPRESS'D.[22]

As Thomas Quayle remarks, there is here "probably no intention or desire to personify at all."[23] Economy of expression is the aim. A slight degree of personification is the inevitable result when, in the interests of condensation, abstract nouns are stripped of the modifiers which usually accompany them. It has been seen how personification was used to particularize the abstract by Warton and Collins. When reading Warton's description of Fancy or Collins's description of Danger, we are invited to forget for the moment the innumerable instances in which these qualities have been a factor in human affairs in favor of the particular embodiment before us. Johnson's lines exemplify the reverse of this process. Johnson's image depends for its effectiveness upon our emotional awareness of the many individual instances in which men of worth have been oppressed by poverty.

Johnson is distinguished among eighteenth-century poets for his masterly use of personification as a means of lending poetic value to the expression of such abstract truths. F. R. Leavis quotes the following lines from the *Vanity of Human Wishes:*

> Yet should thy Soul indulge the gen'rous heat,
> Till captive Science yields her last retreat;
> Should Reason guide thee with her brightest ray,
> And pour on misty Doubt resistless day;
> Should no false Kindness lure to loose delight,
> Nor Praise relax, nor Difficulty fright;
> Should tempting Novelty thy cell refrain,
> And Sloth effuse her opiate fumes in vain;
> Should Beauty blunt on fops her fatal dart,
> Nor claim the triumph of a Letter'd heart;
> Should no Disease thy torpid veins invade,
> Nor Melancholy's phantoms haunt thy shade;
> Yet hope not life from grief or danger free,
> Nor think the doom of man revers'd for thee.[24]

These abstractions are very different from "the common run of poetical abstractions in the period." They have "concrete Force":

They represent not absence of pressure, but concentration; it is as if Johnson were bringing to bear on his verse an irresistible weight of experience—of representative human experience; it is his greatness that he can justify the pretension implicit in the phrase, 'the doom of man,' and invest his generalities with substance.[25]

Some of these abstractions are slightly particularized, but they do not stand alone as if inviting the reader's leisurely inspection:

they are used to lend weight and significance to the truth embodied in the final couplet. If they have "concrete force," it is due to the idea which informs them.

A somewhat different use of personification occurs in Johnson's paraphrase of Proverbs 6:6-11:

> Turn on the prudent Ant thy heedful eyes,
> Observe her labours, Sluggard, and be wise.
> No stern command, no monitory voice
> Prescribes her duties, or directs her choice,
> Yet timely provident, she hastes away
> To snatch the blessings of the plenteous day;
> When fruitful summer loads the teeming plain,
> She gleans the harvest, and she stores the grain.
> How long shall sloth usurp thy useless hours,
> Dissolve thy vigour, and enchain thy powers?
> While artful shades thy downy couch enclose,
> And soft solicitation courts repose,
> Amidst the drowsy charms of dull delight,
> Year chases year, with unremitted flight,
> Till want, now following, fraudulent and slow,
> Shall spring to seize thee like an ambush'd foe.[26]

Much of the impressive quality of the poem is due to the effectiveness of the concluding image. Donald Davie says of this:

The process of beggary is gradual, yet indigence comes on a sudden. Johnson's "spring" is faithful to this painful paradox, as true to his Scripture as to the human experience of the Bankruptcy court.[27]

Davie cites this as an example of "the true personification, the one with the force of metaphor," and finds it "the most important sort of personification" in use among eighteenth-century poets.[28] Personification may be, as B. H. Bronson has said, "radically inseparable from other kinds of metaphor,"[29] but in so far as it approaches the nature of the allegorical description, as it does in the poetry of the Wartons and Collins, it loses metaphorical force. It may have virtues of its own, but these will be the virtues of the allegorical picture rather than the virtues of metaphor. Without attempting any formal distinction between the two sorts of personification, one may say that these Johnsonian abstractions approach nearer to metaphor than do the "ideal forms" of Joseph Warton or William Collins.

Modern criticism has emphasized the nondecorative aspects of metaphor: "Often it [metaphor] constitutes the only possible way by which we can convey the special quality of an experience." Metaphor "is not something external to thinking: it is central."[30] I. A. Richards maintains that thought works basically through metaphor. Richards analyzes the figure into "the tenor (idea) and the vehicle (image): together they constitute the figure; their interaction constitutes the meaning."[31] Johnson's use of the verb "spring" exerts metaphorical force because, through its use, Johnson is able to achieve a perfect interaction between image and idea. In a broader sense, it is possible to say that the passage on "the doom of man" is effective in the way that metaphor is effective. The abstractions constitute the imagery which lends weight to the idea, and the idea, in turn, lends "concrete force" to the imagery.

It has not been usual to regard Johnson as a highly metaphorical poet, but if he does not create new "overt" metaphors, he does vivify abstractions which remain lifeless in the poetry of many of his contemporaries. Macdonald Emslie quotes the following lines from the *Vanity of Human Wishes:*

> Remark each anxious toil, each eager strife,
> And watch the busy scenes of crouded life;
> Then say how hope and fear, desire and hate,
> O'erspread with snares the clouded maze of fate.[32]

The overt metaphors in the last line are not remarkable in themselves, nor are the abstractions in the preceding line, but the final couplet is effective because Johnson does not allow these elements to remain isolated. The abstractions "are connected . . . by *O'erspread, Snares* and *clouded Maze";* these metaphors are used "to enforce the abstractions."[33] The abstract words assume the vitality which metaphor has as a figure conveying "the special quality of an experience." Our impression, as Emslie says, "is that the poet knows what these abstractions amount to in terms of actual life."[34] Emslie contrasts these personifications with the "pretentiously statuesque" figures which appear in Gray's *Ode on a Distant Prospect of Eton College*. The two lines which Gray uses for "Passions" and "Jealousy" in stanza seven "add nothing to the significance of the capitalized words, and the reader can only feel the kind of satisfaction that comes when the entirely expected is completely fulfilled: 'ah yes.' " One does not feel that Gray knows what his abstractions amount to "in terms of actual life." Gray, in this stanza, gives us the conventional "white melancholy" of the period, but Johnson's lines are "the poetry of a sincere religious pessimism."[35]

The final stanza of the ode *On the Death of Mr. Robert Levet* contains another instance of personification which is effectively metaphorical:

> Then, with no throbbing fiery pain,
>   No cold gradations of decay,
> Death broke at once the vital chain,
>   And free'd his soul the nearest way.[36]

"The verb 'broke,' " says Donald Davie, "reaping the cumulative interest and movement of the first two lines, enlivens alike the personification which governs it and the dead metaphor ('the vital chain') which follows."[37] In another instance, "concrete force" is lent to the abstraction by Johnson's manner of describing the object upon which it acts. Johnson is relating the plight of the "sinking statesman." Grub Street has deserted him in favor of "growing names":

> For growing names the weekly scribbler lies,
> To growing wealth the dedicator flies,
> From every room descends the painted face,
> That hung the bright Palladium of the place,
> And smoak'd in kitchens, or in auctions sold,
> To better features yields the frame of gold;
> For now no more we trace in ev'ry line

> Heroic worth, benevolence divine:
> The form distorted justifies the fall,
> And detestation rids th' indignant wall.[38]

The pathetic fallacy in the last line heightens the effect of the abstraction. Detestation stands for the human agency, or agencies, responsible for the removal of the picture; at the same time our sense of the detestation in which the statesman is held is heightened by our feeling that even the wall itself is indignant, and that it actively exerts itself in getting rid of the hated picture. A similar effect is gained in the following passage through the use of ambiguity. Johnson is describing the condition of the elderly sensualist:

> In vain their gifts the bounteous seasons pour,
> The fruit autumnal, and the vernal flow'r;
> With listless eyes the dotard views the store,
> He views, and wonders that they please no more;
> Now pall the tasteless meats, and joyless wines,
> And Luxury with sighs her slave resigns.[39]

There is an ambiguity in the last line which relates "luxury" to "dotard." Luxury is a separate entity—one thinks of the capacity for sensuous enjoyment leaving the dotard—but the phrase "with sighs" particularizes the abstraction; one thinks of the dotard himself pushing away the meats and wines "with sighs." The two readings reinforce each other.

Personified abstractions are often used in the poetry of statement as aids in achieving an effect of completeness. They are particularly noticeable in couplets which sum up the sense of particular passages. At the end of one of the verse paragraphs in his poem on Sir Thomas Hanmer, Johnson uses three of them in a couplet which acts to define the essential character of the man:

> Her gifts despis'd, corruption blush'd and fled,
> And fame pursu'd him [Hanmer], where conviction led.[40]

A better-known example occurs in the Drury Lane *Prologue*. The bards of Charles the Second's day

> . . . proudly hop'd to pimp in future Days.
> Their Cause was gen'ral, their Supports were strong,
> Their Slaves were willing, and their Reign was long;
> Till Shame regain'd the post that Sense betray'd,
> And Virtue call'd Oblivion to her Aid.[41]

Johnson uses four abstractions in describing the fate that over-took the Restoration wits. The abstractions in these couplets lend an air of "spruce finality"[42] to the verse, thereby giving a sense of completeness to the subject under discussion. One feels that Johnson has rounded off the topic, leaving no more to be said. Personification is employed in these instances because it allows the poet to achieve a desirable economy of expression. Its virtues, in this case, are those of epigram. Personification is of great value in lending epigrammatic force since, through its use, the poet is able to say much in little and to say it with suitable impressive-ness. As I. A. Richards says, the economy of expression which is achieved through the use of the figure lends force to the thought: *"emotional impulses"* are not allowed to *"dissipate them-selves."*[43] The couplet quoted from the Drury Lane *Prologue* is one of the best examples of the epigrammatic use of personifica-tion. Johnson has much to say; the fact that it is said in short com-pass lends force to the statement: the emotional impulses of the reader are not allowed to dissipate themselves in the contempla-tion of nonessentials.

The habit of using abstractions in didactic poetry involves dan-gers indicated by Leavis in the phrase "absence of pressure." I have indicated some of the methods employed by Johnson in lending weight to his abstractions. In other instances, Johnson in-vests his abstractions with concrete force by means of what one may call a use of particular reference. A simple example occurs in the passage on Archbishop Laud in the *Vanity:*

> Nor deem, when learning her last prize bestows,
> The glitt'ring eminence exempt from foes;
> See when the vulgar 'scape, despis'd or aw'd,
> Rebellion's vengeful talons seize on Laud.

> From meaner minds, tho' smaller fines content,
> The plunder'd palace, or sequester'd rent;
> Mark'd out by dangerous parts he meets the shock,
> And fatal Learning leads him to the block.[44]

The first couplet states a general proposition: "learning" does not yet have concrete force. The succeeding lines particularize the abstraction, thereby lending weight to the general statement. Learning becomes "fatal Learning" through its association with a particular individual.

With this, one may compare the following couplet from the first paragraph of the *Vanity:*

> How rarely reason guides the stubborn choice,
> Rules the bold hand, or prompts the suppliant voice.[45]

Johnson makes a statement about human reason in general. "Reason," however, does not remain an empty abstraction. Johnson relates it to the activities of particular human types. It is shown in its relation to "the bold hand" and "the suppliant voice." These vivid synecdoches illustrate Johnson's happy precision in the choice of epithet. It may be said generally that such precision is a major factor in lending an effect of concrete force to his use of abstractions. Thus, in the following stanza from the ode to Levet the abstractions are particularized by the epithets "hopeless" and "lonely":

> In misery's darkest caverns known,
> His useful care was ever nigh,
> Where hopeless anguish pour'd his groan,
> And lonely want retir'd to die.[46]

As in the case of "the bold hand" and "the suppliant voice," one feels the particular instance pushing hard at the abstraction. Johnson is able to achieve such an effect because he chooses epithets which "*denote* emotion as well as thought." As W. C. Brown has said, "the emotion communicated by abstract words arises from conceptual meanings . . . the thought itself denotes the emotion."[47] The words "anguish" and "want" are concepts which denote a degree of emotion in themselves, and the emotional effect is further intensified by the use of the conceptual modifiers "hopeless" and "lonely." It may be said in general that when such an effect is achieved through the use of abstract words, the effect on the reader is not different in kind from that which is achieved through particularized description. Crabbe, in his poem *The Village,* describes in detail the circumstances which attend the death of an elderly pauper.[48] Johnson chooses epithets which manage to convey the same impression of unrelieved desolation which Crabbe conveys through his detailed account of the "particular instance."

One of the criticisms which modern readers may be inclined to bring against the eighteenth-century habit of personifying passions and moral principles is that such a practice prevents a valuable discrimination between "different sorts of attitude and outlook." Different types of behavior "must, at a push, be approved alike as 'virtue' or condemned alike as 'vice.' " But the Augustans, as Donald Davie says, were "not concerned with those features which make a man unique, but with those which he has in common with his fellows," and although "the two sorts of concern are different," there "are no *a priori* grounds for thinking one less interesting or less moral than the other."[49] Eighteenth-century personification, even so, does not necessarily function to prevent a full realization of "the many and baffling ways" in which moral principles "exert and display themselves in the world."[50] One may note in proof of this Johnson's *Prologue* to *A Word to the Wise:*

> THIS night presents a play, which publick rage,
> Or right or wrong, once hooted from the stage;
> From zeal or malice, now no more we dread,
> For English vengeance *wars not with the dead.*
> A generous foe regards, with pitying eye,
> The man whom fate has laid, where all must lye.
> To wit, reviving from its author's dust,
> Be kind, ye judges, or at least be just:
> Let no resentful petulance invade

> Th' oblivious grave's inviolable shade.
> Let one great payment every claim appease,
> And him who cannot hurt, allow to please;
> To please by scenes unconscious of offence,
> By harmless merriment, or useful sense.
> Where aught of bright, or fair, the piece displays,
> Approve it only—'tis too late to praise.
> If want of skill, or want of care appear,
> Forbear to hiss—the Poet cannot hear.
> By all, like him, must praise and blame be found;
> At best, a fleeting gleam, or empty sound.
> Yet then shall calm reflection bless the night,
> When liberal pity dignify'd delight;
> When pleasure fired her torch at Virtue's flame,
> And mirth was bounty with an humbler name.[51]

The personifications in the final couplet have been "worked for." The statement that "mirth" is "bounty with an humbler name" is justified by an argument which examines in careful detail the shades and distinctions of moral principle which are relevant to an audience's reaction to a "second-rate play by a dead author":

If Johnson had concluded his poem with 'Be kind, ye judges, or at least be just,' or with 'By harmless merriment or useful sense,' the poem would have been trivial. And for merriment or sense to take capital letters would have been more than the poem could bear. As it is, a dead metaphor comes to life; Bounty is plenitude and bonte (goodness). Mirth is thankful enjoyment of the plenitude of creative providence; it is a compelling and dignified idea.

"Mirth" and "Bounty" assume these valuable meanings because "by the end of the poem Johnson has shown that to be kind is the only way of being just, in the given set of circumstances," and this has been effected by an argument which has discriminated between "different sorts of attitude and outlook."[52]

The uses to which Johnson puts his abstractions are such that the impulse toward visualization, if carried to extremes, is rather a hindrance than a help. Certain of his abstractions are endowed with the sort of descriptive detail which contemporary critics approved of as aids to the formation of vivid mental pictures. The personification of "want" in the paraphrase of Proverbs 6:6-11 is an example. Another occurs in the Drury Lane *Prologue:*

> Existence saw him spurn her bounded Reign,
> And panting Time toil'd after him in vain.[53]

Less vivid, but more fully detailed, is the description of Justice as she existed during "Alfred's golden reign":

> Fair Justice then, without constraint ador'd,
> Held high the steady scale, but deep'd the sword.[54]

A vivid pictorial imagination might perceive these figures as complete spiritual beings. I suggest, however, that the perception of clear and distinct images tends to weaken the force of the personifications. In Johnson's figures, image and idea are usually inseparable; the full effect of the figure depends upon one's apprehension of tenor and vehicle as a unity. One's perception of the vehicle, if carried to the extremes of vivid pictorialization, tends to weaken this effect of unity by diverting attention from the significance of the tenor. The description of Justice provides an illustration. It is possible here to imagine a classical figure similar to the statues of antiquity. Such an image may be helpful, provided one's apprehension of purely pictorial values does not tend to overshadow one's perception of the particular significance of the "deep'd" sword.[55] The image of "want" in the paraphrase of Proverbs 6:6-11 is one of the most vivid in the whole compass of Johnson's verse, but we minimize the effect if we allow the image of something "springing" to fill our imaginations to a point where we tend to overlook the significance of the word "spring" as the verbal reflection of a particular moral paradox. The description of "panting Time" may be an exception. The image is vivid and Johnson's language works directly to enhance the pictorial effect. Nevertheless, it would seem that, for the modern reader at least, the perception of a distinct mental picture in this instance would tend to carry an effect of inappropriate grotesquerie.

Using Johnson as my example, I have tried to show that in the best didactic verse of the eighteenth century the prosopopoeia becomes something more than an "empty abstraction." I have shown in some detail the variety of means used in lending the abstraction that quality of concrete force which gives it poetic value. Among these are various devices of rhetoric such as the use of ambiguity or the establishment of a pathetic fallacy. Or again, there is the reference to something outside the abstraction itself. In such instances, particular individuals or social types become the objects to which the abstraction refers. At the opposite pole, we have in Johnson a direct reliance upon the inherent values of personification as a device of style. The condensation and economy of expression which it promotes are exploited to the full, and the figure becomes a means of achieving a forceful and comprehensive finality of statement. And, above all, one may take note of Johnson's skillful precision in the use of abstract words and epithets which denote emotion. All such elements in Johnson's handling of the personified abstraction subserve the purposes of metaphor. In Johnson's personifications thought works basically through the image; as in metaphor, one finds a close and significant interaction between image and idea.

I have not been concerned here to discuss the other side of the question; that is, what there is about the abstraction *qua* abstraction which made it so popular a figure with eighteenth-century poets. The human mind naturally seeks to master the multifarious details of experience by imposing a certain order upon them, and this involves the formulation of "abstract truths." Personification, however, is only one device among many others which may be used when dealing with the expression of such "truths" in poetry. It is necessary to remember that the frequent use of personified abstractions in eighteenth-century verse is supported by a climate of opinion favorable to the contemplation of the abstraction as such, quite apart from the way in which it is used. The abstraction may have "concrete force," but it will fail of its effect if readers react, as nineteenth-century readers often reacted, with feelings of distaste at the mere mention of personified "virtues" and "vices." The recent studies of B. H. Bronson and E. R. Wasserman have indicated some of the factors which favored the use of personified abstractions in eighteenth-century poetry. I wish to consider the matter more closely in connection with Pope's use of the figure in satire. Such a study will serve three purposes. It will show the peculiar advantages which attach to the use of allegorical figures in satire, and it will provide an opportunity to examine the personified abstraction, not in the isolated contexts in which I have so far examined it, but as it appears in relation to the total structure and content of the poem. Lastly, and most important of all, the study of Pope's satiric verse will illustrate that positive feeling for the abstraction as such which animates the use of the figure in the best neoclassic verse generally.

CHAPTER VII

THE INHERENT VALUES
OF EIGHTEENTH-CENTURY PERSONIFICATION:
POPE

NEAR THE FIGURE of Spleen, writes Pope in the *Rape of the Lock:*

> Two Handmaids wait the Throne: Alike in Place,
> But diff'ring far in Figure and in Face.
> Here stood *Ill-nature* like an *ancient Maid,*
> Her wrinkled Form in *Black* and *White* array'd;
> With store of Pray'rs, for Mornings, Nights and Noons,
> Her Hand is fill'd; her Bosom with Lampoons.
>   There *Affectation* with a sickly Mien
> Shows in her Cheek the Roses of Eighteen,
> Practis'd to Lisp, and hang the Head aside,
> Faints into Airs, and languishes with Pride;
> On the rich Quilt sinks with becoming Woe,
> Wrapt in a Gown, for Sickness and for Show.
> The Fair-ones feel such Maladies as these,
> When each new Night-Dress gives a new Disease.[1]

These figures are presented in "bold relief." They are described with as much elaboration of detail as the figures of Philosophy, Wisdom, or Virtue in Joseph Warton's poem *The Enthusiast*.[2] Pope's figures are much more effective, however, and this is not the result, simply, of superior genius. The fact is that vivid and picturesque detail assumes a more positive function in satiric allegory than it is able to assume in nonsatiric modes of allegorical presentation. When the eighteenth-century poet sets out seriously to present the reader with a number of picturesque allegorical "fictions," he is always in some danger of straining his reader's sense of decorum. The willing suspension of disbelief may be violated: too much detail will make the figures appear grotesque and therefore merely ridiculous.[3] While the element of the grotesque is something to be guarded against when dealing with allegorical figures in nonsatiric verse, it is a positive advantage to the poet using such figures as vehicles for satire. Its effect is to heighten the satire by investing the objects of the poet's scorn with an appearance of the ridiculous. Other things being equal, the greater the accumulation of grotesque detail the more forcible the satire, provided always, of course, that every detail adds point to the satiric message.

Satire allowed the poet more freedom in regard to the physical differentiae of the abstraction. Eighteenth-century satire deals with the universal vices and failings of humanity, but it does so most effectively through the exploitation of contemporary instances. Pope's Ill-nature and Affectation are eighteenth-century figures; the former is the typical old maid, the latter the overly delicate young girl of the period. One feels that Pope has described types peculiar to the eighteenth century, however "universal" the particular vices which they typify. The significance of the figures as symbols is heightened by our feeling that, once again, the particular instance is pushing hard at the abstraction. Satiric allegory is free from one of the major weaknesses inherent in the illustrative mode of allegorical presentation. The poet whose ideal figures simply illustrate the general natures of particular virtues or vices cannot tap the large reservoir of reader-interest which lies open to the poet whose abstract figures are immediately referable to particular instances in real life.

Addison had said that personified abstractions were improper "actors" in an epic poem because "there is not that Measure of Probability annexed to them, which is requisite in Writings of this Kind."[4] Most eighteenth-century poets and critics agreed

with him, but that abstractions could assume an important place
in the structure of an eighteenth-century poem is evident from
the use Pope makes of them in the fourth book of the *Dunciad*.
F. R. Leavis has recently emphasized the importance of the fourth
book. It not only "stands . . . apart from the other books, but
much above them: it is a self-sufficient poem."[5] There is reason
to believe that Pope would have agreed with this judgment. The
fourth book, he says,

may properly be distinguished from the former, by the Name of
the GREATER DUNCIAD, not so indeed in Size, but in Subject.[6]

These words are contained in a humorous note by "Bentley," but
they express an important truth. The subject is great: Pope is describing the apotheosis of moral as well as intellectual perversity.
The satire is on a level of high seriousness; the attack on dull
writers is but one part of a far-reaching analysis of the moral and
intellectual evils which threaten, not only literature, but society
as a whole. The abstractions which figure at the Levee of Dulness
and those which appear in the prophetic vision at the end of the
book are employed as a means of dramatizing the larger issues
which underlie the purely topical satire. Their function is highly
important: they bring home to us, in vivid and concrete fashion,
the cosmic nature of Pope's theme. The theme of the poem is indicated in four lines which immediately precede the description
of the Levee of Dulness:

> Then rose the Seed of Chaos, and of Night,
> To blot out Order, and extinguish Light,
> Of dull and venal a new World to mold,
> And bring Saturnian days of Lead and Gold.[7]

The evils with which Pope deals are of cosmic import. They
are capable of destroying the structure of society as a whole, if
unchecked by the forces of morality and good sense. The description of Dulness mounted on her throne follows:

> She mounts the Throne: her head a Cloud conceal'd,
> In broad Effulgence all below reveal'd,

('Tis thus aspiring Dulness ever shines)
Soft on her lap her Laureat son reclines.
   Beneath her foot-stool, *Science* groans in Chains,
And *Wit* dreads Exile, Penalties, and Pains.
There foam'd rebellious Logic, gagg'd and bound,
There, stript, fair *Rhet'ric* languish'd on the ground;
His blunted Arms by *Sophistry* are born,
And Shameless *Billingsgate* her Robes adorn.
Morality, by her false Guardians drawn,
Chicane in furs, and *Casuistry* in Lawn,
Gasps, as they straiten at each end the cord,
And dies, when Dulness gives her Page the word.
Mad *Mathesis* alone was unconfin'd,
Too mad for mere material chains to bind,
Now to pure Space lifts her extatic stare,
Now running round the Circle, finds it square.
But held in ten-fold bonds the *Muses* lie,
Watch'd both by *Envy's* and by *Flatt'ry's* eye:
There to her heart sad Tragedy addrest
The dagger wont to pierce the Tyrant's breast;
But sober History restrain'd her rage,
And promis'd Vengeance on a barb'rous age.
There sunk Thalia, nerveless, cold, and dead,
Had not her sister Satyr held her head:
Nor cou'd'st thou, CHESTERFIELD! a tear refuse,
Thou wept'st, and with thee wept each gentle Muse.
   When lo! a Harlot form soft sliding by,
With mincing step, small voice, and languid eye;
Foreign her air, her robe's discordant pride
In patch-work flutt'ring and her head aside:
By singing Peers up-held on either hand,
She tripp'd and laugh'd, too pretty much to stand;
Cast on the prostrate Nine a scornful look,
Then thus in quaint Recitativo spoke.[8]

Personification has been defined as "a radical tendency of the human psyche . . . basic to every impulse toward dramatic representation."[9] In the above instance, Pope uses the figure to dramatize the transformations which occur when Dulness infects the arts and sciences which give civilization its value. His own words are the best commentary on the care with which he discriminates particular effects:

Science is only depressed and confined so as to be rendered useless; but *Wit* or *Genius,* as a more dangerous and active enemy, punished or driven away: *Dulness* being often reconciled in some degree with learning, but never upon any terms with Wit. And accordingly it will be seen that she admits something *like* each Science, as Casuistry, Sophistry, etc., But nothing like *Wit, Opera* [the "Harlot form"] alone supplying its place.[10]

The effects of Dulness on Science, Wit, and the rest are sufficiently deplorable, but one notes a more serious effect: Morality dies when Dulness gives the word. This circumstance parallels the extinction of morality when Dulness has finally conquered the earth and "Universal Darkness buries All." Order and light are associated with morality and good sense; the fact that these still exist in some areas of society imposes a precarious order upon those areas dominated by Dulness. It is only when Dulness has conquered all, that order is completely extinguished. When this has happened, it is no longer possible to speak of "something *like* each Science." There is nothing left but "Universal Darkness":

> She comes! she comes! the sable Throne behold
> Of *Night* Primaeval and of *Chaos* old!
> Before her, *Fancy's* gilded clouds decay,
> And all its varying Rain-bows die away.
> *Wit* shoots in vain its momentary fires,
> The meteor drops, and in a flash expires.
> As one by one, at dread Medea's strain,
> The sick'ning stars fade off th'ethereal plain;
> As Argus' eyes by Hermes' wand opprest,
> Clos'd one by one to everlasting rest;
> Thus at her felt approach, and secret might,
> *Art* after *Art* goes out, and all is Night.
> See skulking *Truth* to her old cavern fled,
> Mountains of Casuistry heap'd o'er her head!
> *Philosophy,* that lean'd on Heav'n before,
> Shrinks to her second cause, and is no more.

> *Physic* of *Metaphysic* begs defence,
> And *Metaphysic* calls for aid on *Sense!*
> See *Mystery* to *Mathematics* fly!
> In vain! they gaze, turn giddy, rave, and die.
> *Religion* blushing veils her sacred fires,
> And unawares *Morality* expires.
> For *public* Flame, nor *private,* dares to shine;
> Nor *human* Spark is left, nor Glimpse *divine!*
> Lo! thy dread Empire, CHAOS! is restor'd;
> Light dies before thy uncreating word:
> Thy hand, great Anarch! lets the curtain fall,
> And Universal Darkness buries All.[11]

The two passages are linked together. They constitute major points of emphasis: the first dramatizing the evils of the contemporary situation, the second revealing the condition of things to come if these evils are allowed to multiply. The intervening portion of the poem is an illustrative commentary on the former passage. We are shown specific instances of the degradation of wit and science, with the corresponding exaltation of sophistry, casuistry, and the rest. We are prepared at the same time for the prophetic vision which concludes the poem. The disciples of Dulness gather about her throne to pay homage and to receive her instructions before going forth to "MAKE ONE MIGHTY DUNCIAD OF THE LAND!" Logically, the next portion of the poem should deal with the individual conquests which Dulness makes:

> O Muse! relate (for you can tell alone,
> Wits have short Memories, and Dunces none),
> Relate, who first, who last resign'd to rest;
> Whose Heads she partly, whose completely, blest.[12]

But Pope has prepared us for the omission of this material. The fourth book "is a *scena* in the manner of *The Temple of Fame* rather than a length of story."[13] Pope is not writing a narrative "Progress of Dulness"; he asks only for so much "darkness visible" as "half to show, half veil, the deep Intent."[14] These purposes have been accomplished; it would be unnecessary, and inappropriate in a vision-poem of this type, for Pope to "relate, who first, who last resign'd to rest."

Geoffrey Tillotson maintains that "the famous conclusion, though cleverly sewn on, does not fit Book IV so well as it did Book III," although he admits that "the misjointed construction that might wreck an epic does not wreck what is offered only as a piece of one."[15]

I have a more positive sense of the conclusion as an integral part of the poem. A conclusion similar in essentials to what we actually have is implied at the very beginning:

> Ye Pow'rs! whose Mysteries restor'd I sing,
> To whom Time bears me on his rapid wing,
> Suspend a while your Force inertly strong,
> Then take at once the Poet and the Song.[16]

The "veil" is to be lifted only for a moment; then Chaos is to return again, taking "at once the Poet and the Song." The poet does not stand outside the events he describes; the encroachments of Dulness will have their due effect upon his Muse. Thus, in the lines immediately preceding the concluding passage, Pope represents his Muse as struggling against the opiate effect which accompanies the progress of Dulness. The Muse attempts to relate the particulars of this progress but the empire of Dulness is now too far advanced; the Muse has received the infection:

> In vain, in vain,—the all-composing Hour
> Resistless falls: the Muse obeys the Pow'r.[17]

And the "light-veil" image which opens the poem is paralleled by the "light-curtain" image which concludes it:

> YET, yet a moment, one dim Ray of Light
> Indulge, dread Chaos, and eternal Night!
> Of darkness visible, so much be lent,
> As half to shew, half veil, the deep Intent.
>
> .   .   .
>
> Lo! thy dread Empire, CHAOS! is restor'd;
> Light dies before thy uncreating word;

> Thy hand, great Anarch! lets the curtain fall,
> And Universal Darkness buries All.[18]

Chaos raises the curtain, Chaos must let it fall again.

I have been at some pains to emphasize the key position of the lines on the Levee of Dulness and those which bring the poem to a conclusion, insofar as these passages contribute to the effect of the poem as a unified whole. There is a definite line of progression leading up to the climax of the poem, and Pope's use of abstractions helps to fix the nature of this progression. Those in the first passage relate chiefly to the arts and sciences. They set the stage for the topical satire which is to follow. It is appropriate that the series Science, Wit, Logic, Rhetoric, Morality, Tragedy, and Satire should be less inclusive and less impressive in a moral sense than the series Fancy, Wit, Truth, Philosophy, Physic Metaphysic, Sense, Religion, Morality. The former passage emphasizes the depressed condition of the various arts and sciences; the latter, the utter extinction of all these (*"Art* after *Art* goes out"), and of Truth, Philosophy, and Religion as well. Two of the most striking figures in the former passage are directed against particular abuses—"Mad Mathesis" and the "Harlot form"—but there is none of this in the latter passage; particular abuses are unworthy of mention in a passage which describes the extinction of the "human Spark" itself.

The allegorical figures in these passages take on a functional importance. They are essential to the plan of the poem. The passages which describe them are points of emphasis upon which the structure of the poem as a whole rests. The abstractions contribute to the total effect of high seriousness in so far as they act to emphasize the larger issues which underlie the topical satire.

Pope's manner of treatment varies with his immediate purpose, but, as in Johnson, the methods employed are those which lend "concrete force" to the abstraction. Sometimes the poet can rely upon the reader's awareness of the "particular instance."

The figures of Ill-nature and Affectation in the *Rape of the Lock*
acquire concrete force by their reference to a type of individual
with which every reader is acquainted. The case is somewhat different when the satire is aimed at the perversions of particular arts
or sciences. There are no arts or sciences contemptible in themselves; there are only particular deviations from generally accepted standards of value. Abstract figures aimed at the perversities of particular arts and sciences effect their purpose by appeal-
ing to the reader's knowledge of what the ideal standard of value
should be in each case. The force of the satire depends upon the
skill of the poet in dramatizing the difference between a generally
accepted standard of value and the particular aberration represented by the object of the satire. Mathematics, which should
demonstrate the powers of logic and reason, shows instead a
spirit of illogic and lunacy. Music, which should be manly and
purposive, inspiring men to virtuous deeds, has become, in Italian
opera, meaningless, languid, and effeminate. The accumulation
of particular instances of such perversities in the course of the
fourth book of the *Dunciad* lends weight to the series of generali-
zations with which Pope concludes the poem. If Pope is poetically
justified in saying that Truth, Philosophy, and Mathematics
"turn giddy, rave, and die," it is because the statement is supported by a weight of particular evidence.

But the concluding passage of the fourth book is notable for
qualities of its own not connected with what has gone before.
This passage, like several others in Pope, is remarkable for what
George Sherburn has called a tone of "flaming elevation."[19] This
tone appears again in the *Epilogue to the Satires* where Pope deals
with the triumph of Vice over Virtue:

> *Virtue* may chuse the high or low Degree,
> 'Tis just alike to Virtue, and to me;
> Dwell in a Monk, or light upon a King,
> She's still the same, belov'd, contented thing.
> *Vice* is undone, if she forgets her Birth,

> And stoops from Angels to the Dregs of Earth:
> But 'tis the *Fall* degrades her to a Whore;
> Let *Greatness* own her, and she's mean no more:
> Her Birth, her Beauty, Crowds and Courts confess,
> Chaste Matrons praise her, and grave Bishops bless:
> In golden Chains the willing World she draws,
> And hers the Gospel is, and hers the Laws:
> Mounts the Tribunal, lifts her scarlet head,
> And sees pale Virtue carted in her stead!
> Lo! at the Wheels of her Triumphal Car,
> Old *England's* Genius, rough with many a Scar,
> Dragg'd in the Dust! his Arms hang idly round,
> His Flag inverted trails along the ground!
> Our Youth, all liv'ry'd o'er with foreign Gold,
> Before her dance; behind her crawl the Old!
> See thronging Millions to the Pagod run,
> And offer Country, Parent, Wife, or Son!
> Hear her black Trumpet thro' the Land proclaim,
> That "Not to be corrupted is the Shame."[20]

The tone rises from a quiet dignity of statement to a pitch of burning intensity as Pope describes the apotheosis of Vice. The poet seems to gain an access of power as the vision begins to take form in his mind. The abstractions reveal themselves to him, not as qualities, but as persons; they become living actors in a gorgeous vision which is a compound of Roman triumph, royal coronation, and Tyburn execution.

The emotion in this passage, and in that which concludes the *Dunciad,* is not generated entirely, or perhaps even chiefly, by indignation over specific instances of ill-doing. Even if these passages are read in isolation, it is impossible not to feel the measure of devotion which Pope gives to what Sherburn had called "emotionalized truth."[21] Pope feels, and feels strongly, the denotative force of the abstraction itself. Virtue, Vice, Morality, Truth—these words excite emotion in Pope, and the emotion of the poet is intensified in accordance with the position of the abstraction in the contemporary scale of moral value.

It is entirely appropriate that Pope should personify Virtue and Vice, easily, and with no feeling of self-consciousness. He and his contemporaries believed that it was a relatively simple matter for men of ordinary good sense to separate the good from the evil in any given area of human endeavor. This is not to say that they saw everything in terms of black and white; Tillotson is right when he calls Pope a "vigilant and subtle discriminator of intention and conduct."[22] The portrait of Addison is the classic instance of this in satire. My point, however, is that once the more delicate shades of conduct were distinguished, they were given a precise value in the moral scale. Men thought of a hierarchy of moral values just as they thought of an ascending scale of being in nature.[23] One result of this way of thinking is that particular virtues and vices are often felt to have a sort of existence of their own independent of their particular manifestations in the realm of human activity. Such a mode of apprehension is conducive to personification in poetry. I have discussed this question in connection with the naturalization of the antique as a part of the eighteenth-century setting. Habits of visualization promoted by an acquaintance with allegorical art are accompanied by habits of thought equally conducive to the materialization of the abstract. Before the poet thinks of personifying a particular moral quality, he has thought of it in terms of its relation to a certain hierarchy of moral values. He considers its special quality as an abstraction as well as the particular manifestation of it with which he is immediately concerned. The former consideration is responsible for the fact that abstract terms assume in eighteenth-century thought a certain air of concreteness and solidity which they rarely assume in contemporary thought.[24] Personification represents this solidifying process carried to its logical conclusion. It is a natural consequence of the tendency to discriminate intellectually between the moral quality as a self-existent entity and the particular instance of its activity in the realm of human intention and conduct.

With the exception of a number of professed allegories, poets writing in the central neoclassic tradition do not, as a rule, give their abstractions "any real employment or ascribe to them any material agency."[25] Johnson praised Pope because in the *Rape of the Lock* Pope had invented "a new race of beings, with powers and passions proportionate to their operation." The use of sylphs and gnomes is more effective than the use of abstractions because

> the employment of allegorical persons always excites conviction of its own absurdity; they may produce effects, but cannot conduct actions; when the phantom is put in motion, it dissolves; thus Discord may raise a mutiny, but Discord cannot conduct a march, or besiege a town.[26]

For Johnson, "extensive allegorical personification" is

> an incongruity which defeats the tenets of good taste because it results in a context which is unbelievable. Although Johnson is clearly stirred to adverse judgment by violation of the rules, there is in his statement the more far-reaching implication that such a breach by inviting ludicrous effects, has precipitated an aesthetic failure.[27]

Edward A. Bloom contrasts this distaste for extensive allegorical personification with the practice of medieval poets. He concludes that allegory was at its best during the Middle Ages when "ecumenical values" were "subjective and inward-looking." The inspirational basis for allegory has lost its force as universal values have become "objective, realistic and material."[28] I believe this general thesis to be true. There was certainly an adequate inspirational basis for ascribing "material agency" to allegorical figures during the Middle Ages when abstractions such as the seven cardinal virtues or the seven deadly sins were thought of most often in connection with the great business of personal salvation. These medieval virtues and vices are not to be regarded as abstractions of the intellect; they were thought of as "persons" actively helping or hindering the soul in its ascent to perfection. Their religious significance gave them a more substantial reality in medieval thought than they have ever since been able to as-

sume. When William Langland introduces personified abstractions as "material agents" in *Piers Plowman*—cheek by jowl, so
to speak, with merchants, friars, and beggars—he is simply giving these entities the same importance in literature as they had
in real life. To personify virtues and vices was simply to translate
them from an invisible to a visible part of nature; the translation did not involve the introduction of "fiction" since both
parts of nature were equally "real" to the medieval poet. During
a period when angels, saints, and devils were thought to appear
visibly to men on earth, it required little "suspension of disbelief" to accept the idea of a personified virtue or vice "conducting
a march" or "besieging a town." Since the personified virtue or
vice was not a "fiction of the mind," but a living character, it was
natural for the medieval poet to give it a personality of its own,
that is, to treat it as another actor in his poem, comparable in
every way to his "human" protagonists.

Thus, the medieval church, picturing the world as a place
where vices and virtues struggled for possession of the immortal
soul, was able to give to abstractions a dramatic significance beyond that which they will normally have during periods when
interest is focused upon the manifestations of particular vices
and virtues as they affect men as members of a secular society.
Nevertheless, as I have sought to show in my discussion of Pope,
there still remained, in the eighteenth century, a positive enthusiasm for the abstraction as such, without regard to its possible
manifestations in the realm of human intention and conduct.
Such a feeling is based, however, less upon the perception of
moral values in their relation to the individual soul, as upon a
perception of their importance to the maintenance of a particular
social order. In Pope and Johnson it is the enthusiasm for social
order which gives to the abstraction that air of independent existence which it sometimes assumes. If religious considerations
formerly determined the value of the social order, they are now
only one element (if a principal one) in determining the shape
and value of that ordered society to which the major neoclassic

writers paid homage. Universal values are no longer wholly "subjective and inward-looking"; on the other hand, they are not yet wholly "objective, realistic and material." We now consider the good or bad qualities of our friends chiefly as they affect us, or as they affect other individuals. In the eighteenth century, such qualities were also considered in the light of their effect upon the social structure as a whole. Were they good or bad measured against the social ideal to which men gave general assent? Universal values were "subjective" in so far as they were looked upon as in-dwelling qualities, inherent in any society which aspired to an ordered and harmonious pattern of social relationships. Such values were thought of as a species of cement binding together the various elements of the social structure; invisible though they were, they acquired something of the solidity associated with the outward emblems of that structure—the signs of dress, rank, or even of complexion, which indicated the place of the individual in the social fabric.

In Pope and Johnson one meets with a type of personification which approaches the nature of metaphor. The idea or sentiment is relatively more important than the image through which it is conveyed, or, it would be more accurate to say, one finds it difficult, if not impossible, to contemplate the one apart from the other at the moment of reading. This is as true of the elaborate satirical portrait as it is of the simple abstraction, as true of Pope's "Harlot form" as it is of Johnson's "hopeless anguish." In both cases imagery becomes an instrument for the direct expression of thought and feeling. The case is otherwise with those abstractions which act to illustrate the essential nature of particular arts, qualities, or affections of mind. Here, as John Ogilvie said, "the Original, from which the Copy is drawn, exists in our own mind."[29] We already know what the abstraction is "like"; it only remains for us to compare the poet's representation with our own sense of it. The image, in short, is intended to appeal chiefly to our esthetic sense or to our sense of "fitness." In Johnson and Pope, on the other hand, the appeal is rather to our emotions: the image is intended to "move the affections."[30]

In general, eighteenth-century personifications may be placed in one or the other of two categories in so far as they approach the nature of metaphor or tend to show the characteristics of allegory. Although I have been concerned in this essay to indicate the differences between these two sorts of personification, it is interesting to note that there is a point where extremes meet. It would be difficult to find two eighteenth-century poets who are further apart than Pope and Collins so far as the general character of their verse is concerned, but both poets seem to "see" their abstractions as living figures. However different the elements of thought and feeling which animate Collins's figure of Evening when compared with those elements which vivify the abstractions in the concluding lines of the *Dunciad,* the impression conveyed in both instances is that of living figures which appear "unbidden, and as in vision, before the poet's mental eye." "What the imagination makes," says D. G. James, "is the world to which the deepest and most strenuous life of personality responds, and to which it adapts itself in all its activities."[31] Collins's world of imagination is not that of Pope, but the fact that both men believe intensely in the reality of their different worlds lends to their abstract figures a kind of visionary "truth" which must always appear when such figures represent objects to which "the deepest and most strenuous life of personality responds."

Conclusion

WORDSWORTH, it has been seen, thought of true personification as a figure of rhetoric rather than as a figure of fancy, but the romantic poet's lack of sympathy with the neoclassic poetic tradition as a whole prevented any real understanding of the effects attained through this "rhetorical" use of personification in eighteenth-century verse. Johnson's poem on Proverbs 6:6-11 is described as a "hubbub of words,"[1] a phrase which reflects Wordsworth's distaste for language which seemed to him fundamentally "artificial." The reaction against the meretricious use of the prosopopoeia in the poetry of his own time carried with it a reaction against eighteenth-century "abstractionism" generally.

But if Wordsworth fails to recognize the values of one type of eighteenth-century personification, he was the first to point out certain of the major weaknesses inherent in the poetic tradition which gave rise to the use of the prosopopoeia as a conventional "figure of fancy." The prevailing modes and conventions of later eighteenth-century verse do not make for a use of the figure which is vital in the sense that personification serves meanings which are of serious concern to the poet himself. The figure was a favorite device with those who sought poetry

in the poetical—in specialized (and conventional) sentiments and attitudes representing, as it were, a solemn holiday or Sabbath from the everyday serious.[2]

One must conclude that Addison's adaptation of the principles of Locke's philosophical theory to English literary criticism had unfortunate results so far as the history of eighteenth-century personification is concerned. The Addisonian strain of critical theory led, in the first instance, to a view of imagination-fancy which seemed to offer the poet an escape from what F. L. Lucas has called the "tyranny" of the "reality-principle."[3] But this reality-principle, however tyrannical, was a part of the atmosphere in which eighteenth-century poets moved and had their being. No real "escape" was possible so long as all knowledge was felt to be empirical. I do not wholly agree with D. G. James that "works of imagination" are necessarily those which "compel a strong sense of the real world" (even though "re-created at a new and unique level, and with a novel integrative and imaginative pattern"),[4] but what James says here would seem to apply to much that is best in eighteenth-century poetry. Collins may believe in the reality of his abstractions as creatures of a spirit-world, but Collins is an exception. Personifications become "real" to the eighteenth-century mind when they are felt as dramatizations of the values, affections, or qualities which relate to the activities of man in the empirical world—not when they are projected as figures from a world of vision. When so projected, it was understood that the poet was drawing upon the stores of his own mind; the eighteenth-century reader did not expect the poet to claim a deeper, more profound reality for his figures than the ordinary use of the word "fiction" warranted, nor did he perceive any vital relation between the "bold fictions" of the poet and the actualities of daily life. One may attribute inherent value to the use of allegorical abstractions in medieval poetry because the medieval poet's use of the figure faithfully reflects the deepest realities of the age in which he lived. The same may be said of personification when it appears to reflect the eighteenth-century poet's consciousness of those in-dwelling moral realities which gave meaning to contemporary patterns of social behavior. But the reader is less likely to attribute inherent value to the figure when projected as a "fiction," because, although the poet goes through the motions of attributing substantial reality to his visionary figures, the reader cannot fail to sense his lack of faith in the essential reality of these fabrications as reflections of his own experience. Only Collins makes one feel that such figures truly reflect moments of visionary exaltation, nor can we be expected to experience such a feeling so long as the empirical theory of knowledge acted to limit the degree of willing assent which the poet gave to the idea of praeternatural reality. The use of personified abstractions as figures of vision is never, accordingly, with most eighteenth-century poets, entirely serious, and we as readers cannot contemplate this use of the figure with that degree of serious assent which we give to it when it appears to reflect the poet's concern with "the actualities of life."

The elements of strength and weakness in eighteenth-century personification are the elements of strength and weakness in eighteenth-century verse generally. The successes which the poets achieve with the figure, as well as their failures, are the successes and failures of the eighteenth-century poetic "genius." The adverse critic will have no difficulty in finding instances of personification which seem proof of the unimaginative, conventional quality of much eighteenth-century verse. But when personification is placed in proper perspective, it is clear that it is also a device which gives truly imaginative expression to elements of thought and feeling which reflect that firm sense of actuality which is to be accounted one of the "central virtues of the civilized mind."[5] Far from being, as Wordsworth thought, a device which removes the reader from the world of "flesh and blood," personification, as used by the major Augustan poets, impels "a strong sense of the real world." No other type of metaphor which eighteenth-century poets employ is more effective in conveying a sense of the real worth and dignity of those moral values which determine the patterns of civilized behavior.

Notes

INTRODUCTION

1. Thomas Quayle, *Poetic Diction: A Study of Eighteenth Century Verse*, London, 1924.

2. Bertrand H. Bronson, "Personification Reconsidered," *ELH*, XIV (1947), 163-77.

3. Earl R. Wasserman, "The Inherent Values of Eighteenth-Century Personification," *PMLA*, LXV (1950), 435-36.

4. *Ibid.*, p. 460.

5. Donald Davie, *Purity of Diction in English Verse*, New York, 1953.

6. In particular, to those of Rachel Trickett and M. H. Abrams. See, respectively, "The Augustan Pantheon: Mythology and Personification in Eighteenth-Century Poetry," in *Essays and Studies Collected for the English Association*, VI (1953), 71-86, and *The Mirror and the Lamp: Romantic Theory and the Critical Tradition*, New York, 1953.

7. Davie, *Purity of Diction in English Verse*, p. 40n. I have used the word "rhetorical" as well as "metaphorical" in describing this type of personification. Neither word is wholly satisfactory, but I have been unable to discover a more adequate term.

8. Wordsworth's phrase. See the 1800 preface to the "Lyrical Ballads," *Prose Works*, ed. A. B. Grosart, London, 1876, II, 84.

9. Cf. F. R. Leavis, "English Poetry in the Eighteenth Century," *Scrutiny* (June, 1936), p. 16.

10. The phrase is from John Hughes's "Essay on Allegorical Poetry," in *Critical Essays of the Eighteenth Century 1700-1725,* ed. W. H. Durham, New Haven, 1915, p. 92.

I. Addison and the Empirical Theory
of Imagination

1. Calvin Daniel Yost, Jr., *The Poetry of the Gentleman's Magazine: A Study in Eighteenth-Century Literary Taste*, Philadelphia, 1936, p. 95.

2. The last years of the century do not appear to show any marked decline in the use of the figure. W. C. Brown finds that personification is used "to excess" in the once-popular narrative poems of Samuel Rogers (*The Pleasures of Memory*, 1792), Robert Bloomfield (*The Farmer's Boy*, 1798), and Thomas Campbell (*The Pleasures of Hope*, 1799). Cf. *The Triumph of Form*, Chapel Hill, N.C., 1948, p. 189.

3. R. D. Havens, "Changing Taste in the Eighteenth Century: A Study of Dryden's and Dodsley's Miscellanies," *PMLA*, XLIV (1929), 526. For the statement concerning Dodsley's inclusiveness, see *ibid.*, p. 519.

4. Yost, *The Poetry of the Gentleman's Magazine*, p. 97. Havens finds that the popularity of odes addressed to personified qualities—"which rioted through English verse of the later eighteenth century"—was at its height from 1760 to 1790. His figures show that the rapid decline in popularity which he mentions does not set in until the second decade of the nineteenth century. R. D. Havens, *The Influence of Milton on English Poetry*, Cambridge, Mass., 1922, pp. 441, 469.

5. Yost, *The Poetry of the Gentleman's Magazine*, p. 140.

6. See E. R. Wasserman, "The Inherent Values of Eighteenth-Century Personification," *PMLA*, LXV (1950), 437-40.

7. "Hobbes' Digest of Aristotle's Rhetoric," in *Aristotle's Poetics . . . and Other Classical Writings on Criticism*, ed. T. A. Moxon, Everyman, London, 1947, p. 159.

8. *Ibid.*, p. 158.

9. *The Institutio Oratoria of Quintilian*, trans. H. E. Butler, Loeb Classical Library, London, III (1922), 307. (*Inst.* viii. 6. II.)

10. Cf. Leonard Welsted, *Works*, ed. John Nichols, London, 1787, p. 400; Richard Fiddes, *A Prefatory Epistle concerning Some Remarks to Be Publish'd on Homer's Iliad*, London, 1714, p. 66; Alexander Gerard, *An Essay on Taste*, London, 1759, p. 25; and Edward Burnaby Greene, *Critical Essays*, London, 1770, p. 30.

11. *Longinus: On the Sublime and Sir Joshua Reynolds: Discourses on Art*, translated and edited by Benedict Einarson and Elder Olson, Chicago, 1945, p. 17 and note.

12. John Dennis, *Critical Works*, ed. E. N. Hooker, Baltimore, I (1939), 455. Cited hereafter as Dennis, *Critical Works*.

13. *Ibid.*, I, 69.

14. The "central doctrine" concerning the epic "was set forth by Le Bossu when he described the epic as a narrative which by means of allegory spread abroad a significant treatment of the moral law." Cf. J. W. H. Atkins, *English Literary Criticism: 17th and 18th Centuries*, London, 1951, pp. 12-13.

15. Dennis, *Critical Works*, II (1943), 337.

16. *Ibid.*, p. 363. Dennis's invariable use of the term "fable" to mean "a story with a moral" is based upon his interpretation of Aristotle's use of the word in the *Poetics*. Any poetic fable which does not point a moral is said to be a "mere fiction," whatever the factual truth of the events which it relates. See "Remarks on Prince Arthur," *ibid.*, I, 69.

17. Dennis, *Critical Works*, I, 106.

18. *Ibid.*, p. 45.

19. *Ibid.*, p. 105.

20. *Ibid.*, p. 489.

21. *Ibid.*, II, cxxxiii-cxxxiv.

22. Clarence D. Thorpe, "Addison's Theory of the Imagination as 'Perceptive Response,' " *Papers of the Michigan Academy of Science, Arts and Letters*, XXI (1935), 511 and note.

23. *Ibid.*, p. 530.

24. Wasserman, "The Inherent Values of Eighteenth-Century Personification," *PMLA*, LXV (1950), 439.

25. *Spectator* 421.

26. *Spectator* 411.

27. *Ibid.*

28. *Ibid.*

29. *Spectator* 419.

30. *Ibid.*

31. *Spectator* 279.

32. *Spectator* 357.

33. *Spectator* 273.

34. *Ibid.*

35. *Spectator* 273, 309.

36. Cf. James Paterson, *A Complete Commentary, with Etymological, Explanatory, Critical and Classical Notes on Milton's Paradise Lost*, London, 1744, p. 249; and Thomas Gibbons, *Rhetoric;*

138

NOTES

or, A View of Its Principal Tropes and Figures, London, 1767, p. 356.

37. Cf. John Hughes, "Essay on Allegorical Poetry," in *Critical Essays of the Eighteenth Century,* ed. Durham, p. 95; John Lawson, *Lectures concerning Oratory,* 3d ed., Dublin, 1760, p. 265; James Burnett, Lord Monboddo, *Of the Origin and Progress of Language,* London, III (1786), 150; Samuel Johnson, "Life of Milton," *Works,* Oxford, 1825, VII, 137; Henry Home, Lord Kames, *Elements of Criticism,* 5th ed., Edinburgh, 1774, II, 394-95. As one approaches the nineteenth century, the allegorical objection begins to lose its force. Thomas Green, writing in 1800, praised "the scene betwixt Satan, Sin, and Death" as "transcendently sublime," and thought "the Allegory, to which Addison objects . . . lost amidst such force and vividness and majesty of description, as . . . renders the grandest passages in Homer and Virgil comparatively feeble and dwarfish" (*Extracts from the Diary of a Lover of Literature,* Ipswich and London, 1810, p. 192).

38. *Spectator* 357.

39. *Spectator* 309.

40. *Spectator* 357.

41. Thomas Parnell, *Poems on Several Occasions,* London, 1726, p. 163.

42. Hughes, "Essay on Allegorical Poetry," in *Critical Essays of the Eighteenth Century,* ed. Durham, p. 95.

43. *Ibid.,* p. 92.

44. *Tatler* 100.

45. Wasserman, "The Inherent Values of Eighteenth-Century Personification," *PMLA,* LXV (1950), 446.

46. John More, *Strictures, Critical and Sentimental, on Thomson's Seasons,* London, 1777, p. 111.

47. *Spectator* 419. Cf. Johnson in the "Preface to Shakespeare": "Shakespeare has no heroes; his scenes are occupied only by men, who act and speak as the reader thinks that he should himself have spoken or acted on the same occasion: even where the agency is supernatural, the dialogue is level with life . . . Shakespeare approximates the remote, and familiarizes the wonderful; the event which he represents will not happen, but if it were possible, its effects would, probably, be such as he has assigned" (*Works,* V, 108). Mrs. Montagu thought that Shakespeare had given to the praeternatural element in his poetry "an air of reality which induces 'our imagina-

tions to adopt what our reasons would reject.' " J. W. H. Atkins, *English Literary Criticism*, pp. 259-60.

48. Edward Bysshe, *The Art of English Poetry*, 6th ed., London, 1718, I, sg. A4.

49. Joseph Addison, "Essay on Virgil's Georgics," *Miscellaneous Works*, ed. A. C. Guthkelch, London, 1914, II, 4.

50. Henry Felton, *A Dissertation on Reading the Classics, and Forming a Just Style* [wr. 1709], 5th ed., London, 1753, p. 90.

51. *Ibid.*, p. 89.

52. *Spectator* 411.

53. It was an axiom during the Renaissance "that value attaches to a vast expenditure of labor as such." "The appreciation of art," said Castelvetro, "is the appreciation of difficulties overcome." See K. E. Gilbert and Helmut Kuhn, *A History of Esthetics*, 2d ed., Bloomington, Indiana, 1953, p. 171.

54. Cf. M. H. Abrams, *The Mirror and the Lamp: Romantic Theory and the Critical Tradition*, New York, 1953, pp. 159-67.

55. *Hobbes's Leviathan*, reprinted from the edition of 1651, Oxford, 1943, p. 11.

56. *Ibid.*, pp. 13-15.

57. John Locke, *An Essay concerning Human Understanding*, ed. A. C. Fraser, Oxford, 1894, I, 145-46 (Bk. II, chap. ii, sect. 2).

58. The words "idea" and "image" are usually to be understood as synonymous terms when they occur in passages of philosophical or psychological analysis, whatever their meanings in other contexts. Cf. Alexander Forbes, Baron Pitsligo (*Essays Moral and Philosophical, on Several Subjects*, London, 1734, p. 87): "THE Memory being consider'd as a Register of Things, whether perceived or imagined, these *Things* are usually called *Ideas;* or, in plainer *English, Images. . . ."* Eighteenth-century empirical philosophy assumed, furthermore, that the "sole elements, or 'ideas,' entering into the products" of the poetic imagination were "wholes or parts, literally, of *images*—exact, although fainter replicas of the original perceptions of sense," and that these mental units were "primarily, if not exclusively, visual images, replicas of the objects of sight." Abrams, *The Mirror and the Lamp*, p. 160.

59. Peter Browne, *The Procedure, Extent, and Limits of Human Understanding*, 2d ed., London, 1729, p. 53.

60. Edmund Burke, "A Philosophical Inquiry into the Origin of

Our Ideas of the Sublime and Beautiful," *Works,* London, 1854, I, 58.

61. David Hume, *Enquiry concerning Human Understanding,* ed. L. A. Selby-Bigge, 2d ed., Oxford, 1927, p. 19 (Sect. II). It should not be supposed from this quotation that I am unaware of the basic "anti-empiricist" character of Hume's teaching. Most eighteenth-century philosophers and men of letters believe, with Locke, that the mind is able to reach conclusions in regard to matters of fact which are objectively valid. Sense-experience, they hold, serves as a basis "from which we can inductively extend our knowledge of facts beyond what the senses and memory reveal" (Norman Kemp Smith, *A Commentary to Kant's "Critique of Pure Reason,"* 2d ed., New York, 1950, p. 599). Hume, on the other hand, "by showing that sense-experience cannot by itself yield conclusions which are objectively valid," effectively "destroys the empiricist position" (*ibid.,* p. 601). While this aspect of Hume's teaching may have had something to do with the eventual breakdown of "empirical" theories of poetic imagination, I cannot find that it had any significant effect upon contemporary theorizing, prior, at least, to the time of Coleridge. The subject, however, is one which requires further study.

62. Jean H. Hagstrum, *Samuel Johnson's Literary Criticism,* Minneapolis, 1952, p. 89.

63. *Ibid.,* p. 6; *Boswell's Journal of a Tour to the Hebrides,* ed. F. A. Pottle and C. H. Bennett, New York, 1936, p. 189.

64. Samuel Johnson, "Life of Butler," *Works,* Oxford, 1825, VII, 151. Compare Sir Joshua Reynolds in the second discourse: "Invention, strictly speaking, is little more than a new combination of those images which have been previously gathered and deposited in the memory: nothing can come of nothing: he who has laid up no materials can produce no combinations." And in the seventh discourse we read that "imagination is incapable of producing anything originally of itself, and can only vary and combine those ideas with which it is furnished by means of the senses. . . ." *Longinus: On the Sublime and Sir Joshua Reynolds: Discourses on Art,* ed. Einarson and Olson, Chicago, 1945, pp. 105, 201.

65. Cf. W. K. Wimsatt, Jr., *Philosophic Words: A Study of Style and Meaning in the Rambler and Dictionary of Samuel Johnson,* New Haven, 1948, p. 96.

66. Quotations from Johnson's *Dictionary* are from H. J. Todd's edition (London, 1827).

67. Alexander Gerard, *An Essay on Genius,* London, 1774, pp. 98-102.

68. Gerard, *An Essay on Taste,* London, 1759, p. 167.

69. Henry Home, Lord Kames, *Elements of Criticism,* 5th ed., Edinburgh, 1774, II, 518-19.

70. *Ibid.,* pp. 513-14.

71. *Ibid.,* pp. 511-12.

72. John Aikin, *Essays on Song-Writing: with a Collection of Such English Songs as Are Most Eminent for Poetical Merit,* London, 1810, p. 6.

73. John Aikin, "An Essay on the Poetry of Milton," in *Memoir of John Aikin . . . with a Selection of His Miscellaneous Pieces,* Philadelphia, 1824, p. 186.

74. Dugald Stewart, *Elements of the Philosophy of the Human Mind,* London, 1792, pp. 475-76.

75. *Ibid.,* p. 477.

76. *Ibid.,* p. 478.

77. Abrams, *The Mirror and the Lamp,* p. 161.

78. Hester Lynch Piozzi, *British Synonymy; or, An Attempt at Regulating the Choice of Words in Familiar Conversation,* London, 1794, I, 221.

79. Abrams, *The Mirror and the Lamp,* p. 158.

80. *Ibid.,* pp. 161-62; Stewart, *Elements of the Philosophy of the Human Mind,* p. 475.

81. John Dryden, Preface to "Troilus and Cressida," *Essays,* ed. W. P. Ker, Oxford, 1900, I, 219.

82. D. G. James, *The Life of Reason: Hobbes, Locke, Bolingbroke,* London, 1949, p. 35.

II. The Personified Abstraction as a "Fiction of the Mind"

1. Clarence D. Thorpe, "Addison's Theory of the Imagination as Perceptive Response,'" *Papers of the Michigan Academy of Science, Arts and Letters,* XXI (1935), 514.

2. *Ibid.,* p. 522.

3. Henry Pemberton, *Observations on Poetry, Especially the Epic: Occasioned by the Late Poem upon Leonidas,* London, 1738, p. 76.

4. Joseph Addison, "Essay on Virgil's Georgics," *Miscellaneous Works,* ed. A. C. Guthkelch, London, 1914, II, 4.

5. Edward Bysshe, *The Art of English Poetry,* 1718, I, sg. A4.

6. Bezaleel Morrice, *The Amour of Venus; or, The Disasters of Unlicens'd Love*, London, 1732, p. 3.

7. *Spectator* 420.

8. Sir Joshua Reynolds, *Works*, ed. Edmund Malone, 4th ed., London, 1809, III, 109.

9. Rensselaer W. Lee, "Ut Pictura Poesis: The Humanistic Theory of Painting," *The Art Bulletin*, XXII (1940), 202.

10. *Spectator* 595.

11. William Whitehead, *An Essay on Ridicule*, London, 1753, pp. 57-61.

12. Cicely Davies, "Ut Pictura Poesis," *MLR*, XXX (1935), 160.

13. Jonathan Richardson, *Explanatory Notes and Remarks on Milton's Paradise Lost*, London, 1734, p. 40.

14. *Ibid.*, p. clxxv.

15. *Ibid.*, p. clx.

16. Jonathan Richardson, *A Discourse on the Dignity, Certainty, Pleasure and Advantage of a Connoisseur*, London, 1719, p. 191.

17. E. R. Wasserman, *Elizabethan Poetry in the Eighteenth Century*, "University of Illinois Studies in Language and Literature," Vol. XXXII (1947), p. 95.

18. George Turnbull, *A Treatise on Ancient Painting, Containing Observations on the Rise, Progress, and Decline of That Art amongst the Greeks and Romans*, London, 1740, p. ix.

19. Hannah More, *Works*, Bohn edition, London, 1854, V, 327.

20. Pepys to Hannah More, Sept. 21, 1783, *Memoirs of the Life and Correspondence of Miss Hannah More*, ed. William Roberts, 3d ed., London, 1835, I, 304. The "mute angel" may be, not so much a personification of Attention, as a description of the "socially shy" Fanny Burney (cf. M. G. Jones, *Hannah More*, Cambridge, Eng., 1952, p. 61). If this is true, Pepys's comment is all the more significant as evidence of the eighteenth-century reader's readiness to assume the fact of personification, when, perhaps, the poet did not consciously intend it.

21. John Scott, *Critical Essays on Some of the Poems, of Several English Poets*, London, 1785, p. 205n.

22. Earl R. Wasserman, "The Inherent Values of Eighteenth-Century Personification," *PMLA*, LXV (1950), 457.

23. Joseph Warton, *Essay on the Genius and Writings of Pope*, 4th ed., London, 1782, II, 165.

24. Lines 414-22.

25. Joseph Warton, *Essay on . . . Pope*, I, 29-30.

26. *Ibid.*, II, 33.

27. *Ibid.*, p. 105n.

28. Thomas Warton, *Observations on the Faerie Queene of Spenser*, London, 1754, p. 220.

29. Richard Hurd, *Q. Horatii Flacci Epistola ad Augustum. . . . To Which Is Added, A Discourse concerning Poetical Imitation*, London, 1751, pp. 121-22.

30. *Ibid.*, p. 122.

31. Hildebrand Jacob, *Works*, London, 1735, p. 405.

32. Daniel Webb, *Remarks on the Beauties of Poetry*, London, 1762, p. 79.

33. James Beattie, *Dissertations Moral and Critical*, Dublin, 1783, II, 406n. With most critics, the argument is one of means, not ends. "Description," said Hugh Blair, "when we want to have it vivid and animated, should be in a concise strain. This is different from the common opinion; most persons being ready to suppose, that upon Description a writer may dwell more safely than upon other things, and that by a full and extended Style, it is rendered more rich and expressive. I apprehend, on the contrary, that a diffuse manner generally weakens it. Any redundant words or circumstances encumber the fancy, and make the object we present to it, appear confused and indistinct. . . . The strength and vivacity of description, whether in prose or poetry, depend much more upon the happy choice of one or two striking circumstances, than upon the multiplication of them" (*Lectures on Rhetoric and Belles Lettres*, 7th ed., London, 1798, II, 13-14). Whether his description be "concise" or "extended," the poet is assumed to have as his object the stimulation of a clear-cut "picture" in the mind of the reader.

But, as Wasserman notes ("The Inherent Values of Eighteenth-Century Personification," *PMLA*, LXV [1950], 457), there was a "small opposition" who required obscurity in the personification as necessary for the sublime. Edmund Burke is the most important member of this group of critics. In Milton's personification of Death, says Burke, "all is dark, uncertain, confused, terrible, and [therefore] sublime to the last degree" (*Works*, 1854, I, 90). Thomas Warton, although he usually favors clear and distinct imagery, criticizes Thomas Newton for saying that, in Milton's account of "horror plum'd" (*Paradise Lost*, IV, 989), "Horror is personify'd, and is made the plume of his [Satan's] helmet" (*Paradise Lost*, ed. Thomas Newton, 4th ed., London, 1757, I, 338). But, says Warton, "we have no precise or determinate conception of what Milton

means. And we detract from the sublimity of the passage in endeavoring to explain it, and to give a distinct signification. Here is a
nameless terrible grace, resulting from a mixture of ideas, and a con-
fusion of imagery" (*Poems upon Several Occasions . . . by John
Milton,* ed. Thomas Warton, 2d ed., London, 1791, p. 505).

Similar comments might be cited, but the question of obscurity in
personification is of small importance for the purposes of this book,
chiefly because eighteenth-century poets do not ordinarily attempt the
fabrication of "obscure" personifications in their own verse. They
may admire instances of this in Milton, but if their own personifications are "obscure," this is rarely, if ever, from design.

34. Quoted in William Collins, *Poems,* ed. Walter C. Bronson,
Boston, 1898, p. xxxix, n. 2.

35. Thomas Quayle, *Poetic Diction: A Study of Eighteenth Century Verse,* London, 1924, p. 150.

36. *Adventurer* 97.

37. *Adventurer* 93.

38. *Adventurer* 57.

39. Few poets would attempt to introduce such figures into their
poems, since it was an article of belief in the eighteenth century
that the presentation of such beings in poetry was justified only in
cases where popular belief sanctioned the notion that such creatures
had a real existence in nature. Richard Hurd, speaking of the
praeternatural element in the epic poem, said that "the success of
these fictions will not be great, when they have no longer any footing
in the popular belief: and the reason is, that readers do not usually
do, as they ought, put themselves in the circumstances of the poet, or
rather of those, of whom the poet writes. . . .

"It is also true, that writers do not succeed as well in painting
what they have heard, as what they believe themselves, or at least ob-
serve in others a facility of believing. And on this account I would
advise no modern poet to revive these faery tales in an epic poem"
(*Letters on Chivalry and Romance,* ed. Edith Morley, London, 1911,
p. 101). Hurd is thinking primarily of Ariosto, Spenser, and the
Milton of *Paradise Lost,* but his remarks apply to all "the more sublime and creative poetry" which addresses itself "solely or principally to the Imagination." The poet who writes this sort of poetry
"has . . . a supernatural world to range in. He has Gods, and
Faeries, and Witches at his command. . . ." Hurd believed that
one could still appreciate poetry of this sort provided one made the
necessary suspension of disbelief, but he had no faith that such poetry

could be written in the eighteenth century. Cf. *Letters,* pp. 93-101.

40. Robert Andrews, *Eidyllia; or, Miscellaneous Poems,* Edinburgh, 1757, p. 4.

41. *Ibid.,* p. 3.

42. John Ogilvie, *Britannia: A Natural Epic Poem, in Twenty Books,* Aberdeen, 1801, p. 48.

43. Ogilvie, *Poems on Several Subjects,* London, 1769, I, ci.

44. John Newbery (publisher), *The Art of Poetry on a New Plan,* London, II (1761), 3. This passage and that cited below (see page 41) are not to be found in Newbery's earlier compilations.

45. Warton, *Essay,* I, 68.

46. *Ibid.,* p. 58.

47. *Ibid.,* II, 35-36.

48. Cf. R. D. Havens, "Changing Taste in the Eighteenth Century," *PMLA,* XLIV (1929), 506. George N. Shuster finds that by the year 1726, "the traditional Pindarick had lost caste." *The English Ode from Milton to Keats,* New York, 1940, p. 169.

49. Giles Jacob, *The Poetical Register; or, The Lives and Characters of All the English Poets,* London, 1723, I, xxii.

50. Cf. *Monthly Review,* XXX (January, 1764), 21.

51. Richard Shepherd, *Odes Descriptive and Allegorical,* 2d ed., London, 1761, pp. iii-iv.

52. Norman Maclean, "From Action to Image: Theories of the Lyric in the Eighteenth Century," in *Critics and Criticism: Ancient and Modern,* ed. R. S. Crane, Chicago, 1952, p. 437.

53. *Ibid.,* p. 439.

54. Wasserman, *Elizabethan Poetry in the Eighteenth Century,* p. 94.

55. John Newbery, *The Art of Poetry on a New Plan,* I (1762), 137.

56. John Newbery, *Grammar and Rhetorick, Being the First and Third Volumes of the Circle of the Sciences,* London, 1776, pp. 161-62.

57. Thomas Leland, *A Dissertation on the Principles of Human Eloquence,* London, 1764, p. 26.

58. R. D. Havens, *The Influence of Milton on English Poetry,* Cambridge, Mass., 1922, p. 669.

59. *Ibid.,* p. 441.

60. In *English Poetry of the Eighteenth Century.* ed. Cecil A. Moore, New York, 1935, pp. 595-96. Cited hereafter as Moore, *English Poetry.*

61. Richard Shepherd, *Odes Descriptive and Allegorical*, pp. 32-38.

62. A. S. P. Woodhouse, "Collins and the Creative Imagination," in *Studies in English by Members of University College, Toronto* (Toronto, 1931), p. 96. Havens finds (*Influence of Milton*, p. 457) that "six of Collins's fourteen odes and one of his ten remaining pieces are . . . affected by the plan of [Milton's] octosyllabics, a greater percentage than is found in any other English writer." For the influence of *L'Allegro* and *Il Penseroso* on the odes of Joseph Warton, see *Influence of Milton*, pp. 462-63, 670.

63. Lines 9-21, Moore, *English Poetry*, p. 603.

64. Havens, *Influence of Milton*, p. 670.

65. Cf. lines 200-250, Moore, *English Poetry*, pp. 602-3.

66. Henry Home, Lord Kames, *Elements of Criticism*, 5th ed., Edinburgh, 1774, II, 519.

67. Lines 20-22. This and all subsequent quotations from the poems of Collins and Gray are from *The Poems of Gray and Collins*, ed. Austin Lane Poole and Christopher Stone, 3d ed., Oxford, 1937.

68. A. S. P. Woodhouse, "Collins and the Creative Imagination," in *Studies in English . . . Toronto*, pp. 105, 108-9.

69. Samuel Johnson, "Life of Collins," *Works*, Oxford, 1825, VIII, 401.

70. *Ode on the Poetical Character*, lines 23-40.

71. Collins, *Poetical Works*, ed. Anna Letitia Barbauld, London, 1797, p. xxiv.

72. *Ode on the Poetical Character*, lines 74-76.

73. Joseph Addison, *Spectator* 419.

74. Johnson, "Life of Collins," *Works*, VIII, 401.

75. Lines 1-25.

III. The Personified Abstraction as an "Object of Sight"

1. Joseph Addison, "Dialogues upon the Usefulness of Ancient Medals," *Miscellaneous Works*, ed. A. C. Guthkelch, London, 1914, II, 298.

2. *Ibid.*, p. 300.

3. *Tatler* 97.

4. Shaftesbury, *Characteristics of Men, Manners, Opinions, Times*, ed. J. M. Robertson, London, 1900, II, 45.

5. Cf. Shaftesbury, *Second Characters; or, The Language of Forms,* ed. Benjamin Rand, Cambridge, Eng., 1914, pp. 30-61.

6. John Gilbert Cooper, *Letters concerning Taste,* 2d ed., London, 1771, pp. 52-55.

7. James Moor, "Essay on the Composition of the Picture Described in the Dialogue of Cebes," in *Essays Read to a Literary Society . . . at Glasgow,* Glasgow, 1759, pp. 31-123.

8. Shaftesbury, *Second Characters,* p. 60.

9. Joseph Spence, *Polymetis,* 2d ed., London, 1755, pp. 303-4.

10. *Ibid.,* p. 292.

11. *Ibid.,* p. 306.

12. *Ibid.,* p. 307.

13. Joseph Spence, *An Essay on Mr. Pope's Odyssey,* 3d ed., London, 1747, p. 211.

14. *Adventurer* 63.

15. James Sutherland, *A Preface to Eighteenth Century Poetry,* Oxford, 1948, pp. 141-42.

16. William Shenstone, *Works,* 5th ed., London, 1777, II, 318-19.

17. Pope to Swift, June 2, 1725, *Works of Alexander Pope,* ed. Elwin-Courthope, London, VI (1871), 383-84.

18. John Dyer, "Grongar Hill," lines 117-18 (*Grongar Hill,* ed. R. C. Boys, Baltimore, 1941, p. 83).

19. Joseph Warton, *An Essay on the Genius and Writings of Pope,* 4th ed., London, 1782, I, 36.

20. Hill to Lady Walpole, June 8, 1734, Aaron Hill, *Works,* 2d ed., London, I (1753), 257.

21. Addison, "Dialogues upon . . . Ancient Medals," *Miscellaneous Works,* II, 298.

22. Charles Lamotte, *An Essay upon Poetry and Painting, with Relation to the Sacred and Prophane History,* Dublin, 1745, p. 46.

23. William Gilpin, *Three Essays: On Picturesque Beauty; On Picturesque Travel; and On Sketching Landscape,* 3d ed., London, 1808, p. 10n.

24. Thomas Warton, *Observations on the Faerie Queene of Spenser,* London, 1754, pp. 218-20.

25. John Pinkerton, *Ancient Scottish Poems, Never Before in Print,* London, 1786, II, 366-67.

26. E. R. Wasserman, "The Inherent Values of Eighteenth-Century Personification," *PMLA,* LXV (1950), 456.

27. Cicely Davies, "Ut Pictura Poesis," *MLR,* XXX (1935), 166.

28. Donald Davie, *Purity of Diction in English Verse,* London, 1952, p. 40n.

29. Lines 23-26; quoted in Macdonald Emslie, "Johnson's Satires and 'The Proper Wit of Poetry,'" *The Cambridge Journal,* VII (March, 1954), 347.

30. Emslie, "Johnson's Satires," *The Cambridge Journal,* VII (March, 1954), 348.

31. Davie, *Purity of Diction in English Verse,* p. 40n.

32. Wasserman, "The Inherent Values of Eighteenth-Century Personification," *PMLA,* LXV (1950), 458.

33. William Melmoth, *The Letters of Sir Thomas Fitzosborne, on Several Subjects,* 5th ed., London, 1758, p. 301.

34. Thomas Reid, *Works,* ed. Sir William Hamilton, 4th ed., Edinburgh, 1854, p. 497.

35. Erasmus Darwin, "First Interlude," *The Botanic Garden,* London, 1825, p. 152.

36. Uvedale Price, *Essays on the Picturesque,* London, 1810, I, 220-21.

37. John Ogilvie, *Poems on Several Subjects,* London, 1769, I, cv.

38. Archibald Alison, *Essays on the Nature and Principles of Taste,* Edinburgh, 2d ed., 1811, II, 237. Even the gestures of the orator were supposed to be "characteristic." John Walker devotes some sixty pages of his *Elements of Elocution* to a discussion of the external "signs" of various passions and emotions. Walker is concerned to teach the aspiring orator the proper attitude of body to be assumed when "impersonating" the various passions and emotions to which his discourse gives rise. Walker assumes that each passion has its proper "attitude," and that this will remain the same, no matter who the orator, what the oration, or what the circumstances under which it is delivered. See *Elements of Elocution . . . to Which Is Added, A Complete System of the Passions; Showing How They Affect the Countenance, Tone of Voice, and Gesture of Body, Exemplified by a Copious Selection of the Most Striking Passages of Shakespeare,* 5th ed., London, 1815, pp. 293-354.

39. Bertrand H. Bronson, "Personification Reconsidered," *ELH,* XIV (1947), 164.

40. "Summer," lines 1435-37.

41. Quoted in *The Works of Oliver Goldsmith,* ed. Peter Cunningham, New York, 1881, III, 353. The essay in which this passage occurs "has been shown to be almost certainly not by [Goldsmith]."

Cf. *Cambridge Bibliography of English Literature*, ed. F. W. Bateson, New York, 1941, II, 640.

42. Davie, *Purity of Diction in English Verse*, p. 40n.

43. June E. Downey, *Creative Imagination: Studies in the Psychology of Literature*, New York, 1929, p. 2.

44. *Essay on Man*, lines 117-20.

45. Warton, *Essay on . . . Pope*, II, 87.

46. Thomas Quayle, *Poetic Diction: A Study of Eighteenth Century Verse*, London, 1924, p. 176.

47. *Ibid.*, p. 156.

48. Edmund Burke, "Sublime and Beautiful," *Works*, London, 1854, I, 170.

49. *Ibid.*, p. 173.

50. D. G. James, *The Life of Reason: Hobbes, Locke, Bolingbroke*, London, 1949, p. 232.

51. Burke, *Works*, I, 171.

52. *Ibid.*, p. 170.

53. *Ibid.*, p. 173.

54. Dugald Stewart, *Elements of the Philosophy of the Human Mind*, London, 1792, p. 492.

55. *Ibid.*, p. 495.

56. Cf. J. Middleton Murry, *The Problem of Style*, London, 1952, p. 87.

57. Cf. M. H. Abrams, *The Mirror and the Lamp: Romantic Theory and the Critical Tradition*, New York, 1953, p. 296.

IV. THE VALUES OF ALLEGORICAL PERSONIFICATION: COLLINS AND GRAY

1. Rachel Trickett, "The Augustan Pantheon: Mythology and Personification in Eighteenth-Century Poetry," in *Essays and Studies Collected for the English Association*, VI (1953), 86.

2. *Ibid.*, p. 74.

3. *Ibid.*, p. 86.

4. See above, p. 35.

5. Trickett, "The Augustan Pantheon," in *Essays and Studies Collected for the English Association*, VI (1953), 82.

6. See above, p. 57.

7. "Gray's Elegy," *Times Literary Supplement* (July 27, 1933), p. 501.

8. Samuel Johnson, "Life of Pope," *Works,* Oxford, 1825, VIII, 332.

9. *Ode to Pity,* lines 10-12.

10. I owe this phrase to F. R. Leavis. See "English Poetry in the Eighteenth Century," *Scrutiny* (June, 1936), p. 16.

11. *Hymn to Adversity,* lines 25-32.

12. C. V. Dean, *Aspects of Eighteenth Century Nature Poetry,* Oxford, 1935, p. 8.

13. *The Progress of Poesy,* lines 36-41.

14. *The Bard,* lines 71-76.

15. *The Progress of Poesy,* lines 28-31.

16. Eleanor M. Sickels, *The Gloomy Egoist: Moods and Themes of Melancholy from Gray to Keats,* New York, 1932, p. 46.

17. Lord David Cecil, "The Poetry of Thomas Gray," *Proceedings of the British Academy,* XXXI (1945), 15.

18. *Merchant of Venice,* II, vi, 14-19. Quoted in *Biographia Literaria,* ed. Shawcross, London, 1949, I, 12 (chap. i).

19. Coleridge, *Biographia Literaria,* I, 209.

20. *Ibid.,* p. 12.

21. Deane, *Aspects of Eighteenth Century Nature Poetry,* p. 57.

22. C. V. Deane quoting Edmund Blunden in *ibid.,* p. 9.

23. C. V. Deane in *ibid.*

24. Walter C. Bronson in Collins, *Poems,* Boston, 1898, p. xlv.

25. Lord David Cecil, "The Poetry of Thomas Gray," *Proceedings of the British Academy,* XXXI (1945), 14. The line from Keats is from the third stanza of the *Ode on Melancholy.*

26. *Ode on the Pleasure arising from Vicissitude,* lines 1-8.

27. Deane, *Aspects of Eighteenth Century Nature Poetry,* p. 9.

28. *Ibid.,* p. 57.

29. "Summer," lines 1647-54.

30. John Scott, *Critical Essays on Some of the Poems, of Several English Poets,* London, 1785, p. 353.

31. Alan D. McKillop, "The Romanticism of William Collins," *Studies in Philology,* XX (1923), 2.

32. Mark Van Doren, *John Dryden,* 3d ed., New York, 1946, p. 197.

33. F. R. Leavis, "English Poetry in the Eighteenth Century," *Scrutiny* (June, 1936), p. 14.

34. Cf. Sickels, *The Gloomy Egoist,* chap. ii.

35. Johnson, "Life of Gray," *Works,* VIII, 487.

36. D. H. Steuert, "Thomas Gray," *The Dublin Review* (January, 1945), p. 64.

37. *Elegy,* lines 29-32.

38. See above p. 34.

39. Thomas Quayle, *Poetic Diction: A Study of Eighteenth Century Verse,* London, 1924, pp. 156-57.

40. "Gray's Elegy," *Times Literary Supplement* (July 27, 1933), p. 501.

41. F. R. Leavis, "English Poetry in the Eighteenth Century," *Scrutiny* (June, 1936), p. 16.

42. *Ibid.,* p. 13.

43. William Wordsworth, Preface (1800) to "Lyrical Ballads," *Prose Works,* ed. A. B. Grosart, London, 1876, II, 84. The reader will note that the following chapter omits consideration of the personified abstraction as it appears in the verse of Burns, Blake, and Cowper. The two former poets, I feel, could be studied more profitably in a monograph dealing with personification in romantic poetry. I am less happy about the omission of Cowper. Wordsworth, however, was not thinking of Cowper when he condemned the use of the personified abstraction, and since the following chapter is concerned with the factors which led to the widespread use of precisely that mode of personification to which Wordsworth objected, it is not felt that the omission of Cowper is as unfortunate as it might at first seem.

V. ATTITUDES TOWARD PERSONIFICATION
IN THE LATE EIGHTEENTH CENTURY: DARWIN AND WORDSWORTH

1. William Hayley, *The Triumphs of Temper; a Poem,* 6th ed., London, 1788, p. v.

2. Thomas J. Mathias, *The Pursuits of Literature,* 7th ed., London, 1798, pp. 31-32. Havens notes the many parodies of the mid- and late-century ode and the adverse comment which not infrequently appeared in the reviews (R. D. Havens, *The Influence of Milton on English Poetry,* Cambridge, Mass., 1922, pp. 467-69). There were many readers, evidently, who "saw quite as clearly as we do to-day the failure of the lyric efforts of the later eighteenth century."

3. W. J. Courthope, *A History of English Poetry,* London, VI (1925), 51.

4. Hayley, *Triumphs of Temper,* p. x.

5. In his *Baviad* (1794) and *Maeviad* (1795).

6. Cf. Dwight L. Durling, *Georgic Tradition in English Poetry*, New York, 1935, pp. 103-4. The *Botanic Garden*, said Coleridge, was, for some years, "greatly extolled, not only by the *reading* public in general, but even by those, whose genius and natural robustness of understanding enabled them afterwards to act foremost in dissipating these 'painted mists' that occasionally rise from the marshes at the foot of Parnassus" (*Biographia Literaria*, ed. J. Shawcross, London, 1949, I, 11-12 [chap. i]). Keats thought it "no mean gratification to become acquainted [in 1816] with Men who in their admiration of Poetry do not jumble together Shakespeare and Darwin." Keats to Charles Cowden Clarke, Oct. 9, 1816, *Letters of John Keats*, ed. M. B. Forman, 3d ed., London, 1948, p. 7.

7. Preface to Margaret Ashmun's *The Singing Swan: An Account of Anna Seward*, New Haven, 1931, p. ix.

8. Joseph Addison, "Essay on Virgil's Georgics," *Miscellaneous Works*, ed. A. C. Guthkelch, London, 1914, II, 4.

9. Cf. M. H. Abrams, *The Mirror and the Lamp: Romantic Theory and the Critical Tradition*, New York, 1953, p. 86.

10. William Whitehead, *A Charge to the Poets*, London, 1762, pp. 16-17.

11. Cf. *Notes and Queries*, CXCVII (1952), 294.

12. Abrams, *The Mirror and the Lamp*, p. 288.

13. Whitehead, *A Charge to the Poets*, p. 17.

14. Abrams, *The Mirror and the Lamp*, p. 86.

15. Joseph Warton, *Adventurer* 57.

16. Cf. Collins, *Poetical Works*, ed. Anna Letitia Barbauld, London, 1797, pp. iii-v.

17. Vicesimus Knox, *Works*, London, 1824, III, 232.

18. Anna Seward to Dr. Downman, March 15, 1792, *Letters of Anna Seward*, Edinburgh, 1811, III, 121.

19. John Aikin, "An Essay on the Poetry of Goldsmith," in *Memoir of John Aikin . . . with a Selection of His Miscellaneous Pieces*, Philadelphia, 1824, p. 302.

20. Cf. Abrams, *The Mirror and the Lamp*, p. 289.

21. Wordsworth's phrase. See below, p. 95.

22. *Boswell's Life of Johnson*, ed. Hill-Powell, Oxford, II (1934), 351-52.

23. Cf. Collins, *Poetical Works*, pp. v-vi.

24. Wordsworth, *Prose Works*, ed. A. B. Grosart, London, 1876, II, 89.

25. *Biographia Literaria,* ed. J. Shawcross, London, 1949, II, 12 (chap. xiv).

26. Wordsworth, *Prose Works,* II, 84.

27. *Ibid.,* p. 92.

28. *Ars Poetica,* lines 343-44.

29. Abrams, *The Mirror and the Lamp,* p. 21.

30. For a detailed consideration of the distinction between "pragmatic" and "expressive" theories of art, see Abrams, *The Mirror and the Lamp,* pp. 14-26.

31. *Ibid.,* p. 23.

32. See below, p. 92.

33. Alexander Schomberg, *Bagley; a Descriptive Poem. With the Annotations of Scriblerus Secundus: to Which Are Prefixed by the Same, Prolegomena on the Poetry of the Present Age,* Oxford, 1777.

34. *Ibid.,* p. 2.

35. *Ibid.,* p. 31.

36. Cf. John Ogilvie, *Poems on Several Subjects,* London, 1769, I, ci, cv. I have found no critic, at least, who discusses the subject at greater length.

37. Ogilvie, *Britannia: A Natural Epic Poem, in Twenty Books,* Aberdeen, 1801, p. 48.

38. Ogilvie, *Providence, an Allegorical Poem,* Boston, 1766, p. 132 (Bk. III, lines 37-42).

39. Cf. Erasmus Darwin, "Advertisement," *Botanic Garden,* London, 1825, p. v.

40. Anna Seward, *Memoirs of the Life of Dr. Darwin,* Philadelphia, 1804, pp. 94-95.

41. *Ibid.,* p. 188.

42. Cf. E. R. Wasserman, "The Inherent Values of Eighteenth-Century Personification," *PMLA,* LXV (1950), 435-36.

43. Darwin, "First Interlude," *Botanic Garden,* p. 151.

44. A simile, said Darwin, "should have so much sublimity, beauty, or novelty, as to interest the reader; and should be expressed in picturesque language, so as to bring the scenery before his eye" ("Interlude II," *Botanic Garden,* p. 162). "Picturesqueness" is not a quality of the thing itself (as are sublimity, beauty, and novelty); Darwin's use of the term "picturesque" has reference merely to his belief that whatever the poet describes should be presented in such a way that the reader will have a vivid mental "picture" of it. For the specialized theories of picturesque landscape developed by Mason and Gilpin, see, respectively, Durling, *Georgic Tradition in English Poetry,* pp.

79-80; and H. F. Clark, *The English Landscape Garden*, London, 1948, p. 32.

Later, in the notes to *The Temple of Nature* (published posthumously, 1803), "by adding to the elements of taste the picturesque, a newfangled notion, Darwin brings himself up to date and makes his bow to the ultra-modernists of his day" (James Venable Logan, *The Poetry and Aesthetics of Erasmus Darwin*, Princeton, 1936, p. 54). See the notes to line 230, canto III; line 160, canto IV; and note XIII of the "Additional Notes" *(The Temple of Nature*, London, 1824, pp. 38, 50-51, 85. This poem is bound with *The Botanic Garden* [London, 1825]).

45. Logan, *The Poetry and Aesthetics of Erasmus Darwin*, p. 78.

46. In the "First Interlude" *(Botanic Garden,* p. 152), Darwin says that "in poetry the personification or allegoric figure is generally indistinct, and therefore does not strike us so forcibly as to make us attend to its improbability; but in painting, the figures being all much more distinct, their improbability becomes apparent, and seizes our attention to it." But distinctness is a comparative matter. Darwin's "allegoric" figures are at least as distinct as those in other eighteenth-century poets. Anna Seward said, truly enough *(Memoirs,* p. 232), that Darwin's description of the "moments" ("Loves of the Plants," II, 191-94) was "obnoxious to his own criticism in the first Interlude" because these beings were "too distinctly described." The poet, indeed, might succeed better with the description of certain phenomena than the painter, but this did not alter the fact that both poet and painter attempted to stimulate "interesting trains of ideas" through the description of visible objects. Cf. "First Interlude," *Botanic Garden*, p. 153.

47. Logan, *The Poetry and Aesthetics of Erasmus Darwin*, pp. 138-39.

48. Darwin, "Loves of the Plants," III, 439-44, *Botanic Garden*, p. 173.

49. Seward, *Memoirs,* pp. 84-85.

50. Darwin, "Loves of the Plants," II, 191-94, *Botanic Garden,* p. 157.

51. Seward, *Memoirs,* p. 232.

52. Darwin, "Advertisement," *Botanic Garden*, p. v.

53. Darwin, *Botanic Garden*, p. 151.

54. Gibbon's remark in chapter IX of *The Decline and Fall of the Roman Empire* (Modern Library ed., New York, n.d., I, 201) is well known: "Among a polished people, a taste for poetry is rather an

amusement of the fancy than a passion of the soul." Lesser writers were in general agreement. John Gregory says in 1766 that "it is a sentiment that very universally prevails, that poetry is a light kind of reading, which one takes up only for a little amusement, and that therefore it should be so perspicuous as not to require a second reading" (Sir William Forbes, *An Account of the Life and Writings of James Beattie*, London, 1824, I, 73). John Aikin takes it for granted that poetry is addressed to the "many" who feel rather than to the "few" who reason (*Memoir of John Aikin*, Philadelphia, 1824, p. 247), and Joseph Priestley maintains that "poetry and works of fiction make a high *entertainment*, when they are made nothing more of; but they make a very poor and insipid *employment*" (*A Course of Lectures on Oratory and Criticism*, London, 1777, p. 144).

55. Wordsworth, *Prose Works*, II, 89.

56. *Ibid.*, p. 100.

57. *Ibid.*, p. 89.

58. *Ibid.*, p. 93.

59. *Ibid.*, p. 86n.

60. *Ibid.*, p. 91.

61. *Ibid.*, p. 92.

62. *Ibid.*, pp. 91-92.

63. *Ibid.*, p. 84.

VI. PERSONIFICATION AS A FIGURE OF RHETORIC: JOHNSON

1. John Dryden, Preface to "Annus Mirabilis," *Essays*, ed. W. P. Ker, Oxford, 1900, I, 15.

2. T. S. Eliot, *The Use of Poetry and the Use of Criticism*, London, 1950, p. 60.

3. J. W. H. Atkins, *English Literary Criticism: 17th and 18th Centuries*, London, 1951, p. 54.

4. M. W. Bundy, "Imagination," in *Dictionary of World Literature*, ed. Joseph T. Shipley, New York, 1953.

5. Pope to Swift, Dec. 19, 1734, *Works of Alexander Pope*, ed. Elwin-Courthope, VII (1871), 330.

6. Alexander Pope, *Imitations of Horace*, ed. John Butt, London, 1939, p. 95.

7. Geoffrey Tillotson, *On the Poetry of Pope*, 2d ed., Oxford, 1950, p. 167.

8. Austin Warren, *Alexander Pope as Critic and Humanist,* "Princeton Studies in English No. I," Princeton, 1929, chap. iv.

9. Pope, *Prose Works,* ed. Norman Ault, Oxford, 1936, p. 226.

10. *Ibid.,* p. 237.

11. Pope, Postscript to the "Odyssey," *Complete Poetical Works,* ed. Henry W. Boynton, Boston, 1931, p. 639.

12. Jean H. Hagstrum, *Samuel Johnson's Literary Criticism,* Minneapolis, 1952, p. 89.

13. *Ibid.,* p. 90.

14. Cf. *ibid.,* pp. 90-91.

15. Johnson, "Rasselas," *Works,* Oxford, 1825, I, 293.

16. Hagstrum, *Johnson's Literary Criticism,* p. 161, n. 28.

17. Johnson, "Life of Milton," *Works,* VII, 130.

18. Hagstrum, *Johnson's Literary Criticism,* p. 94.

19. *Ibid.,* p. 93. W. R. Keast reaches a similar conclusion. Poetic genius for Johnson, he finds, "is merely the sum of all the powers of the mind operating with maximum effect; the separate ingredients of reason, imagination, fancy, judgment, are less important than their combination; and the separate work or materials of each counts for less than the total vigor of mind which can discover and represent 'the whole system of life' in both its regularity and variety" ("The Theoretical Foundations of Johnson's Criticism," in *Critics and Criticism: Ancient and Modern,* ed. R. S. Crane, Chicago, 1952, p. 404).

20. George Sherburn (ed.), *The Best of Pope,* New York, 1946, p. xxxviii.

21. Horace Gregory, *The Shield of Achilles: Essays on Beliefs in Poetry,* New York, 1944, p. 17.

22. *London,* lines 177-78.

23. Thomas Quayle, *Poetic Diction: A Study of Eighteenth Century Verse,* London, 1924, p. 141.

24. Lines 143-56; F. R. Leavis, *Revaluation,* New York, 1947, p. 117.

25. Leavis, *Revaluation,* p. 118.

26. Johnson, *Poems,* ed. David Nichol Smith and Edward L. McAdam, Oxford, 1941, pp. 151-52.

27. Donald Davie, *Purity of Diction in English Verse,* New York, 1953, p. 39.

28. *Ibid.,* pp. 39, 40n.

29. Bertrand H. Bronson, "Personification Reconsidered," *ELH,* XIV (1947), 166.

30. Cleanth Brooks and Robert Penn Warren, *Modern Rhetoric*, New York, 1949, p. 419.

31. "Metaphor," in *Dictionary of World Literature*, ed. Shipley.

32. Lines 3-6; Macdonald Emslie, "Johnson's Satires and 'The Proper Wit of Poetry,'" *The Cambridge Journal*, VII (March, 1954), 352.

33. Emslie, "Johnson's Satires," *The Cambridge Journal*, VII (March, 1954), 352.

34. *Ibid.*

35. *Ibid.*

36. Lines 33-36.

37. Davie, *Purity of Diction in English Verse*, p. 39.

38. *The Vanity of Human Wishes*, lines 81-90.

39. *Vanity*, lines 261-66.

40. Lines 33-34.

41. Lines 24-28.

42. I borrow the phrase which Mark Van Doren uses to characterize the effect of the heroic couplet. Cf. *John Dryden*, 3d ed., New York, 1946, p. 69.

43. I. A. Richards, *Practical Criticism*, New York, 1951, pp. 200-201.

44. Lines 165-72.

45. Lines 11-12.

46. Lines 17-20.

47. Wallace Cable Brown, *The Triumph of Form*, Chapel Hill, N.C., 1948, pp. 78-79.

48. Book I, lines 262-345.

49. Cf. Davie, *Purity of Diction in English Verse*, pp. 44-45.

50. *Ibid.*, p. 46.

51. *Poems*, ed. Smith and McAdam, pp. 61-62.

52. Cf. Davie, *Purity of Diction*, pp. 46-47.

53. Lines 5-6.

54. *London*, lines 251-52.

55. Cf. Smith's and McAdam's note (*Poems of Samuel Johnson*, p. 22): "Johnson's intention was to show Justice in her traditional posture, holding the sword with the point resting on the ground or pointing downwards; she suspended punishment, for which there was no need in a golden age, but she did not give up her power to punish."

158

NOTES

VII. The Inherent Values
of Eighteenth-Century Personification:
Pope

1. Canto IV, lines 25-38, *The Rape of the Lock and Other Poems,* ed. Geoffrey Tillotson, London, 1940, pp. 182-83.

2. See above, pp. 44-45.

3. Wasserman, noting the objections to the grotesque element in Spenser's personifications, concludes that the neoclassicists "considered it ill-bred and puerile to read with willing suspension of disbelief" (*Elizabethan Poetry in the Eighteenth Century,* "University of Illinois Studies in Language and Literature," Vol. XXXII (1947), p. 98). This would seem to be particularly true of the early part of the century, when the popular belief in witchcraft and "similar occult phenomena" sometimes led to "hideous outbreaks of superstition." Anything out-of-the-way would be suspect: the eighteenth century, it has been said, "held, precariously enough, to its newly won sanity." Such a feeling might well lead to a prejudice against the extravagant and the "unnatural" in literature, as in life. Cf. James Sutherland, *A Preface to Eighteenth Century Poetry,* Oxford, 1948, pp. 6-7.

4. *Spectator* 273.

5. F. R. Leavis, *The Common Pursuit.* London, 1952, p. 91. George Sherburn believes the fourth book "probably" the last poem Pope wrote, and finds it a fitting culmination to his poetic career: "Pope's sense of intellectual values, expressed many times in his career, he here restates with a solemn sincerity and a relative lack of personal animus that is fitting in a final poetic achievement. This solemnity is seen in the opening lines and in the famous conclusion. . . . The fourth Book is not a contradiction of the first three Books: it is a richer and more imaginative restatement of the values announced in 1728 and 1729." "The Dunciad, Book IV," *Studies in English,* Dept. of English, Univ. of Texas, 1944, Austin, 1945, pp. 174, 189-90.

6. *The Dunciad,* ed. James Sutherland, London, 1943, p. 339. All references to Pope's *Dunciad* are to this edition.

7. Lines 13-16.

8. Lines 17-52.

9. Bertrand H. Bronson, "Personification Reconsidered," *ELH,* XIV (1947), 166.

10. George Sherburn (ed.), *The Best of Pope,* New York, 1946, p. 333.

11. Lines 629-56.

12. Lines 619-22.

13. Geoffrey Tillotson, *On the Poetry of Pope*, 2d ed., Oxford, 1950, p. 59.

14. Lines 3-4.

15. Tillotson, *On the Poetry of Pope*, p. 58.

16. Lines 5-8.

17. Lines 627-28.

18. Lines 1-4, 653-56.

19. Sherburn, *Best of Pope*, p. xxxii.

20. Lines 137-60, *Imitations of Horace*, ed. John Butt, London, 1939, pp. 308-9.

21. Sherburn, *Best of Pope*, p. xxxiv.

22. Tillotson, *On the Poetry of Pope*, p. 42.

23. Cf. Josephine Miles (*Wordsworth and the Vocabulary of Emotion*, "University of California Publications in English," Vol. XII, Berkeley, 1942, p. 87): "Simply, the eighteenth century's use of the term *emotion* (with its alternative terms) differed from ours and others in some major characteristics: one being that it was a definite term with definite boundaries in the scale of human functions; another, that with all its main phases it was held to be the same in all men, consequently the more definite; and a third that, since it was so plain, both statement of it and exterior manifestation of it could have an accepted meaning and value, so that it was heartily given place in all the surfaces of expression and action."

24. Compare, for instance, the quality of the language which John Lawson uses in criticizing the contemporary faculty-psychology of mind. The operations of mind, says Lawson, are popularly "looked upon as several independent Principles, distinct Beings, grafted as it were into the Mind, and acting by their own Force. How else shall a common Reader think of *Conscience,* when he meets with it supporting various Characters: Now it is a Judge, then an Accuser; at one Time an Advocate, at another a Witness; it hath a Bar, a Tribunal, is armed with Lashes and Scorpions?" (*Lectures concerning Oratory*, 3d ed., Dublin, 1760, p. 153). The faculty-psychology, by emphasizing the powers and functions of various distinct qualities of mind, undoubtedly did much to further this process of "solidification."

25. Cf. Edward A. Bloom, "The Allegorical Principle," *ELH*, XVIII (1951), 184.

26. Johnson, "Life of Pope," *Works*, Oxford, 1825, VIII, 332.

160   NOTES

27. Bloom, "The Allegorical Principle," *ELH*, XVIII (1951), 183.

28. *Ibid.*, p. 190.

29. John Ogilvie, *Poems on Several Subjects*, London, 1769, I, cv.

30. Cf. M. H. Abrams, *The Mirror and the Lamp: Romantic Theory and the Critical Tradition*, New York, 1953 (p. 16): Horace's *"prodesse* and *delectare* . . . together with another term introduced from rhetoric, *movere*, to move, served for centuries to collect under three heads the sum of aesthetic effects" which poetry was thought to have upon the reader.

31. D. G. James, *Scepticism and Poetry: An Essay on the Poetic Imagination*, London, 1937, p. 49.

CONCLUSION

1. Wordsworth, Appendix (1802) to the preface to the "Lyrical Ballads," *Prose Works*, ed. A. B. Grosart, London, 1876, II, 104.

2. F. R. Leavis, "English Poetry in the Eighteenth Century," *Scrutiny* (June, 1936), pp. 23-24.

3. F. L. Lucas, *The Decline and Fall of the Romantic Ideal*, Cambridge, Eng., 1937, p. 98.

4. D. G. James, *Scepticism and Poetry: An Essay on the Poetic Imagination*, London, 1937, p. 49.

5. Cf. F. R. Leavis, "English Poetry in the Eighteenth Century," *Scrutiny* (June, 1936), pp. 23-24.

Bibliography of Works Cited

Abrams, M. H. The Mirror and the Lamp: Romantic Theory and the Critical Tradition. New York, Oxford University Press, 1953.

Addison, Joseph. Miscellaneous Works, ed. A. C. Guthkelch. 3 vols., London, 1914.

Adventurer. London, 1825.

Aikin, John. Essays on Song-Writing; with a Collection of Such English Songs as Are Most Eminent for Poetical Merit.

———Memoir of John Aikin, M.D. by Lucy Aikin. With a Selection of His Miscellaneous Pieces, Biographical, Moral and Critical. Philadelphia, 1824.

Alison, Archibald. Essays on the Nature and Principles of Taste. 2d ed., 2 vols., Edinburgh, 1811.

Andrews, Robert. Eidyllia; or, Miscellaneous Poems . . . with a HINT to the British Poets. Edinburgh, 1757.

Aristotle's Poetics . . . and Other Classical Writings on Criticism, ed. T. A. Moxon. Everyman, London, J. M. Dent, 1947.

Ashmun, Margaret. The Singing Swan: An Account of Anna Seward and Her Acquaintance with Dr. Johnson, Boswell, and Others of Their Time. New Haven, Yale University Press, 1931.

Atkins, J. W. H. English Literary Criticism: 17th and 18th Centuries. London, Methuen, 1951.

Beattie, James. Dissertations Moral and Critical. 2 vols., Dublin, 1783.

Blair, Hugh. Lectures on Rhetoric and Belles Lettres. 7th ed., 3 vols., London, 1798.

Bloom, Edward A. "The Allegorical Principle," ELH, XVIII (1951), 163-90.

Boswell, James. Journal of a Tour to the Hebrides with Samuel

Johnson, ed. F. A. Pottle and C. H. Bennett. New York, Literary
    Guild, 1936.
———Life of Johnson, ed. G. B. Hill, rev. L. F. Powell. 6 vols.,
    Oxford, Clarendon Press, 1934-50.
Bowers, R. H. "Pure Poetry in 1762," *Notes and Queries,* CXCVII
    (1952), 294.
Bronson, Bertrand H. "Personification Reconsidered," *ELH,* XIV
    (1947), 163-77.
Brooks, Cleanth, and Robert Penn Warren. Modern Rhetoric. New
    York, Harcourt Brace, 1949.
Brown, Wallace Cable. The Triumph of Form: A Study of the Later
    Masters of the Heroic Couplet. Chapel Hill, N.C., University
    of North Carolina Press, 1948.
Browne, Peter. The Procedure, Extent, and Limits of Human Un-
    derstanding. 2d ed., London, 1729.
Burke, Edmund. Works. Bohn's British Classics, 6 vols., London,
    1854.
Burnett, James (Lord Monboddo). Of the Origin and Progress of
    Language. 2d ed., Vol. III, London, 1786.
Bysshe, Edward. The Art of English Poetry. 6th ed., 2 vols., London,
    1718.
Cambridge Bibliography of English Literature, ed. F. W. Bateson.
    Vol. II, New York, Macmillan, 1941.
Cecil, Lord David. "The Poetry of Thomas Gray," Proceedings of
    the British Academy, Vol. XXXI. London, Geoffrey Cumberlege,
    1945.
Clark, H. F. The English Landscape Garden. London, Pleiades
    Books, 1948.
Coleridge, Samuel Taylor. Biographia Literaria, ed. J. Shawcross. 2
    vols., London, Oxford University Press, 1949.
Collins, William. Poems, ed. Walter C. Bronson. Boston, 1898.
———Poetical Works, ed. Anna Letitia Barbauld. London, 1797.
Cooper, John Gilbert. Letters concerning Taste . . . to Which Are
    Added, Essays on Similar and Other Subjects. 2d ed., London,
    1771.
Courthope, W. J. A History of English Poetry. 6 vols., London,
    1904-25.
Critical Essays of the Eighteenth Century 1700-1725, ed. Willard
    Higley Durham. New Haven, 1915.
Darwin, Erasmus. The Botanic Garden, a Poem in Two Parts; Con-

taining the Economy of Vegetation and the Loves of the Plants. London, 1825.

———The Temple of Nature; or, The Origin of Society: A Poem. London, 1824.

Davie, Donald. Purity of Diction in English Verse. New York, Oxford University Press, 1953.

Davies, Cicely. "Ut Pictura Poesis," *MLR*, XXX (1935), 159-69.

Deane, C. V. Aspects of Eighteenth Century Nature Poetry. Oxford, Blackwell, 1935.

Dennis, John. Critical Works, ed. E. N. Hooker. 2 vols., Baltimore, Johns Hopkins Press, 1939-43.

Dictionary of World Literature, ed. Joseph T. Shipley. New York, Philosophical Library, 1953.

Downey, June E. Creative Imagination: Studies in the Psychology of Literature. New York, Harcourt Brace, 1929.

Dryden, John. Essays, ed. W. P. J. Ker. 2 vols., Oxford, 1900.

Durling, Dwight L. Georgic Tradition in English Poetry. New York, Columbia University Press, 1935.

Dyer, John. Grongar Hill, ed. Richard C. Boys. Baltimore, Johns Hopkins Press, 1941.

Eliot, T. S. "Johnson's 'London' and 'The Vanity of Human Wishes,'" in English Critical Essays: Twentieth Century. World Classics, London, Oxford University Press, 1950, pp. 301-10.

———The Use of Poetry and the Use of Criticism. London, Faber and Faber, 1950.

Emslie, Macdonald. "Johnson's Satires and 'The Proper Wit of Poetry,'" *The Cambridge Journal*, VII (March, 1954), 347-60.

Felton, Henry. A Dissertation on Reading the Classics, and Forming a Just Style. 5th ed., London, 1753.

Fiddes, Richard. A Prefatory Epistle concerning Some Remarks to Be Publish'd on Homer's Iliad: Occasioned by the Proposals of Mr. Pope towards a New English Version of That Poem. London, 1714.

Forbes, Sir William. An Account of the Life and Writings of James Beattie, LL.D. 2 vols., London, 1824.

Gerard, Alexander. An Essay on Genius. London, 1774.

———An Essay on Taste. London, 1759.

Gibbon, Edward. The Decline and Fall of the Roman Empire. Vol. I, Modern Library, New York, n.d.

Gibbons, Thomas. Rhetoric; or, A View of Its Principal Tropes and Figures, in Their Origin and Powers. London, 1767.

Gifford, William. The Baviad, and the Maeviad. 6th ed., London, 1800.

Gilbert, Katharine Everett, and Helmut Kuhn. A History of Esthetics. Bloomington, Ind., Indiana University Press, 1953.

Gilpin, William. Three Essays: On Picturesque Beauty; On Picturesque Travel; and On Sketching Landscape: with a Poem, On Landscape Painting. 3d ed., London, 1808.

Goldsmith, Oliver. Works, ed. Peter Cunningham. 4 vols., New York, 1881.

"Gray's Elegy." (London) *Times Literary Supplement* (July 27, 1933), 501-2.

Green, Thomas. Extracts from the Diary of a Lover of Literature. Ipswich and London, 1810.

Greene, Edward Burnaby. Critical Essays. London, 1770.

Gregory, Horace. The Shield of Achilles: Essays on Beliefs in Poetry. New York, Harcourt Brace, 1944.

Hagstrum, Jean H. Samuel Johnson's Literary Criticism. Minneapolis, University of Minnesota Press, 1952.

Havens, Raymond Dexter. "Changing Taste in the Eighteenth Century: A Study of Dryden's and Dodsley's Miscellanies," *PMLA*, XLIV (1929), 501-36.

————The Influence of Milton on English Poetry. Cambridge, Harvard University Press, 1922.

Hayley, William. The Triumphs of Temper; a Poem: in Six Cantos. 6th ed., London, 1788.

Hill, Aaron. Works. 2d ed., 4 vols., London, 1753-54.

Hobbes, Thomas. Leviathan. Reprinted from the edition of 1651. Oxford, Clarendon Press, 1943.

Home, Henry (Lord Kames). Elements of Criticism. 5th ed., 2 vols., Edinburgh, 1774.

Hume, David. Enquiries concerning the Human Understanding and concerning the Principles of Morals, ed. L. A. Selby-Bigge. 2d ed., Oxford, Clarendon Press, 1927.

Hurd, Richard. Letters on Chivalry and Romance with the Third Elizabethan Dialogue, ed. Edith Morley. London, 1911.

————Q. Horatii Flacci Epistola ad Augustum. . . . To Which Is Added, A Discourse concerning Poetical Imitation. London, 1751.

Jacob, Giles. The Poetical Register; or, The Lives and Characters of All the English Poets. 2 vols., London, 1723.

Jacob, Hildebrand. Works . . . containing Poems on Various Subjects, and . . . Several Pieces in Prose. London, 1735.

James, D. G. The Life of Reason: Hobbes, Locke, Bolingbroke. London, Longmans Green, 1949.

———Scepticism and Poetry: An Essay on the Poetic Imagination. London, Allen and Unwin, 1937.

Johnson, Samuel. A Dictionary of the English Language, ed. H. J. Todd. 3 vols., London, 1827.

———Poems, ed. David Nichol Smith and Edward L. McAdam. Oxford, Clarendon Press, 1941.

———Works. 9 vols., Oxford, 1825.

Jones, M. G. Hannah More. Cambridge, Cambridge University Press, 1952.

Keast, W. R. "The Theoretical Foundations of Johnson's Criticism," in Critics and Criticism: Ancient and Modern. Chicago, University of Chicago Press, 1952, pp. 389-407.

Keats, John. Letters, ed. Maurice Buxton Forman. 3d ed., Oxford, Oxford University Press, 1948.

Knox, Vicesimus. Works. 7 vols., London, 1824.

Lamotte, Charles. An Essay upon Poetry and Painting, with Relation to the Sacred and Prophane History. Dublin, 1745.

Lawson, John. Lectures concerning Oratory. 3d ed., Dublin, 1760.

Leavis, F. R. The Common Pursuit. London, Chatto and Windus, 1952.

———"English Poetry in the Eighteenth Century," Scrutiny (June, 1936), 13-31.

———Revaluation: Tradition and Development in English Poetry. New York, George W. Stewart, 1947.

Lee, Rennselaer. "Ut Pictura Poesis: The Humanistic Theory of Painting," The Art Bulletin, XXII (1940), 197-269.

Leland, Thomas. A Dissertation on the Principles of Human Eloquence: with Particular Regard to the Style and Composition of the New Testament. London, 1764.

Locke, John. An Essay concerning Human Understanding, ed. A. C. Fraser. 2 vols., Oxford, 1894.

Logan, James Venable. The Poetry and Aesthetics of Erasmus Darwin. Princeton, Princeton University Press, 1936.

Longinus: On the Sublime and Sir Joshua Reynolds: Discourses on Art. Translated and edited by Benedict Einarson and Elder Olson. Chicago, Packard, 1945.

Lucas, F. L. The Decline and Fall of the Romantic Ideal. Cambridge, Cambridge University Press, 1937.

McKillop, Allan D. "The Romanticism of William Collins," *SP*, XX (1923), 1-16.

Maclean, Norman. "From Action to Image: Theories of the Lyric in the Eighteenth Century," in Critics and Criticism: Ancient and Modern. Chicago, University of Chicago Press, 1952, pp. 408-60.

Mathias, Thomas James. The Pursuits of Literature. 7th ed., London, 1798.

Melmoth, William. The Letters of Sir Thomas Fitzosborne, on Several Subjects. 5th ed., London, 1758.

Miles, Josephine. Wordsworth and the Vocabulary of Emotion. University of California Publications in English, vol. XII, No. 1, Berkeley, 1942.

Monthly Review, XXX (January, 1764), 21.

Moor, James. Essays Read to a Literary Society . . . at Glasgow. Glasgow, 1759.

Moore, Cecil A. (ed.). English Poetry of the Eighteenth Century. New York, Henry Holt, 1935.

More, John. Strictures, Critical and Sentimental, on Thomson's Seasons. London, 1777.

Morrice, Bezaleel. The Amour of Venus; or, The Disasters of Unlicens'd Love. London, 1732.

Murry, J. Middleton. The Problem of Style. London, Oxford University Press, 1952.

Newbery, John. The Art of Poetry on a New Plan. 2 vols., London, 1761-62.

————Grammar and Rhetorick, Being the First and Third Volumes of the Circle of the Sciences. London, 1776.

Newton, Thomas (ed.). Paradise Lost. 4th ed., 2 vols., London, 1757.

Ogilvie, John. Britannia: A Natural Epic Poem, in Twenty Books. Aberdeen, 1801.

————Poems on Several Subjects. 2 vols., London, 1769.

————Providence, an Allegorical Poem. Boston, 1766.

Parnell, Thomas. Poems on Several Occasions. London, 1726.

Paterson, James. A Complete Commentary, with Etymological, Explanatory, Critical and Classical Notes on Milton's Paradise Lost. London, 1744.

Pemberton, Henry. Observations on Poetry, Especially the Epic: Occasioned by the Late Poem upon Leonidas. London, 1738.

Pinkerton, John. Ancient Scotish Poems, Never Before in Print. 2 vols., London, 1786.

Piozzi, Hester Lynch. British Synonymy; or, An Attempt at Regulating the Choice of Words in Familiar Conversation. 2 vols., London, 1794.

Pitsligo, Alexander Forbes. Essays Moral and Philosophical, on Several Subjects. London, 1734.

Poems of Gray and Collins. Ed. Austin Lane Poole and Christopher Stone. 3d ed., London, Oxford, 1937.

Pope, Alexander. Complete Poetical Works, ed. Henry W. Boynton. Boston, Houghton Mifflin, 1931.

————The Dunciad, ed. James Sutherland. London, Methuen, 1943.

————An Essay on Man, ed. Maynard Mack. London, Methuen, 1950.

————Imitations of Horace, with An Epistle to Dr. Arbuthnot and the Epilogue to the Satires, ed. John Butt. London, Methuen, 1939.

————Prose Works, ed. Norman Ault. Oxford, Basil Blackwell, 1936.

————The Rape of the Lock and Other Poems, ed. Geoffrey Tillotson. London, Methuen, 1940.

————Works, ed. W. Elwin and W. J. Courthope. 10 vols., London, 1871-89.

Price, Uvedale. Essays on the Picturesque, as Compared with the Sublime and the Beautiful; and, On the Use of Studying Pictures, for the Purpose of Improving Real Landscape. 3 vols., London, 1810.

Priestley, Joseph. A Course of Lectures on Oratory and Criticism. London, 1777.

Quayle, Thomas. Poetic Diction: A Study of Eighteenth Century Verse. London, Methuen, 1924.

Quintilian. Institutio Oratoria, trans. H. E. Butler. Loeb Classical Library, Vol. III, London, William Heineman, 1922.

Reid, Thomas. Works, ed. Sir William Hamilton. 4th ed., Edinburgh, 1854.

Richards, I. A. Practical Criticism: A Study of Literary Judgment. New York, Harcourt Brace, 1951.

Richardson, Jonathan. A Discourse on the Dignity, Certainty, Pleasure and Advantage, of the Science of a Connoisseur. London, 1719.

Richardson, Jonathan, and Son. Explanatory Notes and Remarks on Milton's Paradise Lost. London, 1734.

Roberts, William (ed.). Memoirs of the Life and Correspondence of Mrs. Hannah More. 3d ed., 4 vols., London, 1835.

Schomberg, Alexander Crowcher. Bagley; a Descriptive Poem. Oxford, 1777.

Scott, John. Critical Essays on Some of the Poems, of Several English Poets. London, 1785.

Seward, Anna. Letters . . . Written between the Years 1784 and 1807. 6 vols., Edinburgh, 1811.

——Memoirs of the Life of Dr. Darwin, Chiefly during his Residence in Lichfield, with Anecdotes of His Friends, and Criticisms on His Writings. Philadelphia, 1804.

Shaftesbury, Anthony Ashley Cooper, third earl of. Characteristics of Men, Manners, Opinions, Times, ed. John M. Robertson. 2 vols., London, 1900.

——Second Characters; or, The Language of Forms, ed. Benjamin Rand. Cambridge, Eng., 1914.

Shenstone, William. Works, in Verse and Prose. 5th ed., 3 vols., London, 1777.

Shepherd, Richard. Odes Descriptive and Allegorical. 2d ed., London, 1761.

Sherburn, George (ed.). The Best of Pope. Revised edition, New York, Ronald Press, 1946.

——"The Dunciad, Book IV." Studies in English, Dept. of English, Univ. of Texas, 1944, Austin, 1945, pp. 174-90.

Shuster, George N. The English Ode from Milton to Keats. New York, Columbia University Press, 1940.

Sickels, Eleanor M. The Gloomy Egoist: Moods and Themes of Melancholy from Gray to Keats. New York, Columbia University Press, 1932.

Smith, Norman Kemp. A Commentary to Kant's "Critique of Pure Reason." 2d ed., New York, Humanities Press, 1950.

Spectator. Everyman, 4 vols., London, J. M. Dent, 1950.

Spence, Joseph. An Essay on Mr. Pope's Odyssey. 3d ed., London, 1747.

——Polymetis; or, An Enquiry concerning the Agreement between the Works of the Roman Poets, and the Remains of the Antient Artists. 2d ed., London, 1755.

Steuert, Dom Hilary. "Thomas Gray," The Dublin Review (January, 1945), pp. 61-67.

Stewart, Dugald. Elements of the Philosophy of the Human Mind. London, 1792.

Sutherland, James. A Preface to Eighteenth Century Poetry. Oxford, Clarendon Press, 1948.

Tatler. 4 vols., London, 1822.

Thomson, J. A. K. Classical Influences on English Poetry. London, Allen and Unwin, 1951.

Thomson, James. Complete Poetical Works, ed. J. Logie Robertson. London, Oxford University Press, 1951.

Thorpe, Clarence DeWitt. "Addison's Theory of Imagination as 'Perceptive Response.'" Papers of the Michigan Academy of Science, Arts and Letters, XXI (1935), 509-30.

Tillotson, Geoffrey. On the Poetry of Pope. 2d ed., Oxford, Clarendon Press, 1950.

Trickett, Rachel. "The Augustan Pantheon: Mythology and Personification in Eighteenth-Century Poetry," in Essays and Studies Collected for the English Association, VI (1953), 71-86.

Turnbull, George. A Treatise on Ancient Painting, Containing Observations on the Rise, Progress, and Decline of That Art amongst the Greeks and Romans. London, 1740.

Van Doren, Mark. John Dryden: A Study of His Poetry. 3d ed., New York, Henry Holt, 1946.

Walker, John. Elements of Elocution. 5th ed., London, 1815.

Warren, Austin. Alexander Pope as Critic and Humanist. Princeton Studies in English No. I, Princeton, Princeton University Press, 1929.

Warton, Joseph. An Essay on the Genius and Writings of Pope. 4th ed., 2 vols., London, 1782.

Warton, Thomas. Observations on the Faerie Queene of Spenser. London, 1754.

Warton, Thomas (ed.). Poems upon Several Occasions, English, Italian, Latin, with Translations, by John Milton. 2d ed., London, 1791.

Wasserman, Earl R. Elizabethan Poetry in the Eighteenth Century. University of Illinois Studies in Language and Literature, Vol. XXXII, Nos. 2-3. Urbana, University of Illinois Press, 1947.

————"The Inherent Values of Eighteenth-Century Personification," PMLA, LXV (1950), 435-63.

Webb, Daniel. Remarks on the Beauties of Poetry. London, 1762.

Welsted, Leonard. Works, ed. John Nichols. London, 1787.

Whitehead, William. A Charge to the Poets. London, 1762.

————An Essay on Ridicule. London, 1753.

Wimsatt, W. K., Jr. Philosophic Words: A Study of Style and Meaning in the Rambler and Dictionary of Samuel Johnson. New Haven, Yale University Press, 1948.

Woodhouse, A. S. P. "Collins and the Creative Imagination: A Study in the Critical Background of his Odes (1746)," in Studies in English by Members of University College, Toronto: Toronto, 1931, pp. 59-130.

Wordsworth, William. Prose Works, ed. Alexander B. Grosart. 3 vols., London, 1876.

Yost, Calvin Daniel, Jr. The Poetry of the Gentleman's Magazine: A Study in Eighteenth-Century Literary Taste. Philadelphia, University of Pennsylvania, 1936.

Index